THE IDEAS OF LE CORBUSIER

THE IDEAS OF
LE CORBUSIER
ON ARCHITECTURE
AND
URBAN PLANNING

Texts edited and presented by
Jacques Guiton
Translation by
Margaret Guiton

George Braziller
New York

Published in the United States in 1981 by
George Braziller, Inc. with the permission of the
Fondation Le Corbusier, Paris.

© 1981 Fondation Le Corbusier

For information address the publisher:

George Braziller, Inc.
One Park Avenue
New York 10016

Library of Congress Card Catalog Number 80-70993

ISBN 0-8076-1004-6 (cloth)
ISBN 0-8076-1005-4 (paper)

Designed by Dana Levy

Contents

To Gordon Bunshaft who,
with Le Corbusier, showed me what
architecture is all about.

Acknowledgements

Acknowledgement is due to the Fondation Le Corbusier, which authorized me to use the writings of Le Corbusier and encouraged me to write this book.

I should like to express, again, my gratitude to my wife, who not only translated Le Corbusier's difficult text but also advised me on the organization of the book.

Mr. Stephen A. Kliment FAIA, architect and editorial consultant, who reviewed the translation of the introduction and the first chapter, contributed constructive comments. Mrs. Catherine Hill reviewed the entire manuscript and made many valuable suggestions.

I was greatly helped by the editorial advice of Miss Letitia O'Connor of George Braziller, Inc.

Foreword

LE CORBUSIER expressed himself in several ways: by building, drawing, painting, writing, and, of course, speaking. One might suppose that drawing was his principal medium, for he has left us thousands of personal drawings, 32,000 architectural and urban plans that were drawn up in his office, and almost a hundred sketchbooks. Drawing certainly came naturally to him, for as he shaped his ideas in his mind, he expressed his thoughts in his drawings.

But the shapes that he created are not gratuitous; his mode of thinking was always linked with our natural environment, with natural forces, with men, women, and children, with communal as well as individual existence, with history, social changes, active forces, movements of ideas, and presentiments of future developments. His entire work as an architect and urban planner is at heart an attempt to propose a certain way of life, to discover our full human potential and reveal it through his architecture.

Such an architecture cannot be fully explained by drawings. It proceeded from ideas, not simply intellectual ideas, but ideas that had been personally tested and experienced. And these ideas had to be expressed in words. Drawings were not enough. Language, which directly communicates with other people, was also necessary. Le Corbusier had to write.

Drawings are less capable of eliciting responses than writings. A book presents questions and expects answers. It attempts to reach out to and communicate with others.

And so Le Corbusier wrote books throughout his life. He wrote, but he also drew. He drew sketches in his books. He wrote on the margins of his sketches. The end result is about forty books, which have been translated into several languages. This is not a series of didactic works, academic treatises, or methodical analyses. It's an explosion of ideas: observations, personal sensations, and arguments involving emotions that Le Corbusier had experienced, difficulties that he had overcome. We cannot simply understand his books; we have to surrender to them, resonate, in the acoustical sense, with their vibrations, the ebb and flow of his thinking.

From the point of view of a rigid rationalist, these books can be bewildering. They contain contradictions, arising out of Le Corbusier's constant search for the different facets of ideas. They are often disorganized. At times we have to decipher them, as though we were clearing a fertile wilderness.

Jacques Guiton, who is an architect, has thus rendered a great service in undertaking the important work presented here: that of selecting Le Corbusier's key passages and of reordering and juxtaposing them so as to help us grasp this outpouring of ideas—ideas that shape human existence on this planet and lead on to the poetry of life.

> Some drawings talk about ideas.
> Some ideas draw shapes.

We must read Le Corbusier's books to understand the reasoning behind his drawings, plans, and buildings, a type of reasoning, sometimes intuitive but always rigorous, that underlies his entire work. This book will greatly help us to do so.

And we must study his plans and drawings, as well as his buildings, to understand his books. None can be isolated from the others. They form an indivisible whole. The thinking of a man.

André Wogenscky
Fondation Le Corbusier, Paris

Introduction

FOR MANY YEARS I have felt that this book should exist and that I would like to write it. Born and trained as an architect in France, in 1948 I moved to New York, where I have since lived, practicing architecture. When I first came to this country, I realized that I was severely handicapped by my ignorance of contemporary architecture. I therefore bought a number of Le Corbusier's books and studied closely his ideas, which I found extremely enlightening.

These ideas, so helpful to me, are presented here in a more organized and compact form than my initial readings and are offered with the hope that they will be of help to other architects and students. I am happy that, after thirty years, I have found the time to complete this project.

Few architects have written as much as Le Corbusier. In 1955 he said that he had written forty-five books,* most of which were already out of print. Some had been translated into English, Spanish, German, Japanese, and, before 1930, Russian. As he explained:

"I wrote not because I enjoyed putting words on paper but because of the enormous complexity of our profession. Driven by a consuming passion and unable to build during the depression of 1929, Hitler's threat of 1933–39, war until 1944, the aftermath of war until 1947, etc., I made drawings and had others make them for me. This produced an incredible number of studies, plans of cities, public buildings and private dwellings, solutions to the problem of automobiles versus pedestrians, which fill five large volumes of the *Oeuvre complète, Le Corbusier, 1910–1952.*

"And what could not be drawn was spoken in lectures given in every continent over a period of thirty years—lectures that were always improvised, hence militant and creative, lectures addressed to audiences friendly, sceptical, or hostile.

---

* Le Corbusier probably included the two series of books on his work published respectively by Girsberger in Zurich and Albert Morancé in Paris.

"And when I was not speaking, I would write down my ideas on paper, one after the other, and this produced a great many books." (32, p. 107)

Many of Le Corbusier's writings have not been translated into English, and the French editions of both his books and the numerous articles that he contributed to journals and essay collections are sometimes difficult to obtain. Like his lectures, they are "militant" and, given his zeal to win over a reluctant public, repetitious. His ideas, set down as they occurred to him, are not always presented systematically. As he himself, speaking of his book *La Ville radieuse (The Radiant City),* explains:

"One must realize that the lives of active pioneers are agitated, crowded, tumultuous. I said so in the opening pages of this book: it is not a serene work, composed in the quiet of a writer's study. Serenity is not my lot, alas!" (11, p. 200)

"It is the result of fifteen years of work; it is crammed with ideas; it is like a larder stuffed with food. I have been criticized for this. But even today I am incapable of setting up an elegant drawing room where etiquette rules supreme." (13, p. 1)

I have attempted to present Le Corbusier's ideas on architecture and urban planning in a condensed and orderly form. However, I have presented only those ideas that may be of use to architects, future architects, and others interested in the subject. I have omitted most references to Le Corbusier's biography, his attacks on the "Academy," and his angry responses to the insults and injustices to which he was so long subjected.

I thought initially of describing Le Corbusier's ideas in my own words but soon realized that he would speak much more effectively for himself. This book thus consists mainly of quotations from his many books and articles, arranged according to subject matter.

I have used the following system of references: The source of any quotation taken from a book by Le Corbusier is given by two numbers: the first is the code number of the book as indicated in the chronological list on page xxx; the second refers to the page number. The sources of quotations taken from his articles or from chapters he contributed to essay collections appear as footnotes.

Le Corbusier often used his own sketches in his publications. These sketches, sometimes hastily drawn during his lectures, form an integral part of the text and are reproduced here. I also show photographs and plans of buildings when these clarify Le Corbusier's ideas.

It is my hope that this book will convey Le Corbusier's ideas to a wider public, correct certain misconceptions, and perhaps encourage the reader to go back to the primary sources. This seems in keeping with Le Corbusier's openhanded attitude toward his ideas:

"In 1923 Mallet-Stevens told me: 'We ought to patent our ideas or at least protect them with trademarks.'

"Certainly not! It is in the nature of ideas to belong to everybody. There are two choices: to give ideas or to take ideas. We do both, really; we gladly give out our ideas; in return we use, we exploit for our own special purposes, ideas scattered through all areas—ideas which one day, in whole or in part, end up helping us. Ideas are public property. To share one's ideas, well, there is simply no other way!" (9, p. 237)

Books by Le Corbusier

This list does not include pamphlets, magazine articles, books to which Le Corbusier contributed chapters, or books published in limited editions.

The date preceding the book's title is the date of the first edition. If a book has been reprinted, the publisher and date of the last reprint are indicated. If a book has been translated, the English title is given in parentheses.

1 1912 **Etude sur le mouvement de l'art décoratif en Allemagne.** Da Capo Press, New York, 1968.

2 1918 **Après le cubisme.**

3 1923 **Vers une architecture.** Editions Arthaud, Paris, 1977. (Towards a New Architecture)

4 1925 **La Peinture moderne.**

5 1925 **L'Art décoratif d'aujourd'hui.** Editions Arthaud, Paris, 1978.

6 1925 **Urbanisme.** Editions Arthaud, Paris, 1980. (The City of Tomorrow and Its Planning)

7 1926 **Almanach d'architecture moderne.**

8 1928 **Une Maison—un palais.** Bottega d'Erasmo, 1976.

9 1930 **Précisions sur un état présent de l'architecture et de l'urbanisme.** Vincent, Fréal & Cie., Paris, 1960.

10 1932 **Croisade ou le crépuscule des académies.**

11 1935 **La Ville radieuse.** Vincent, Fréal & Cie., Paris, 1964.(The Radiant City)

12 1935 **Aircraft.**

13 1937 **Quand les cathédrales étaient blanches.** Collection Médiations Denoël, Paris, 1977. (When Cathedrals Were White)

14 1938 **Des Canons, des munitions? merci! des logis . . . S.V.P.**

15 1939 **Le Lyrisme des temps nouveaux et l'urbanisme.**

For further details see the bibliography page 119

CHAPTER I
What Is Architecture?

LE CORBUSIER first expressed his ideas about architecture in the journal *L'Esprit nouveau,* which he founded with Amédée Ozenfant in 1920. The journal, published by the two founders with the poet Paul Dermée, appeared irregularly—twenty-eight issues in all—until 1925.

Twelve of Le Corbusier's numerous *L'Esprit nouveau* articles deal with architecture. In 1923 he republished these, with an added chapter, "Architecture or Revolution," as the book *Vers une architecture"* (*Towards a New Architecture*).

This book contains Le Corbusier's entire theory of architecture. His later writings merely restate, with greater refinement and clarity, the ideas set forth in *Vers une architecture.*

Drawing on these sources, I have chosen those passages that provide the clearest and most complete view of Le Corbusier's ideas. They are, for the most part, arranged thematically, rather than chronologically.

Le Corbusier's answer to the question "What is architecture?" cannot be given in a single sentence. It is composed of a cluster of definitions, explanations, and examples without which we cannot accurately express his thinking. Despite his much quoted and often misinterpreted phrase "a house is a machine for living," Le Corbusier, unlike most of the leading architects of his day, distinguished sharply between esthetic and functional considerations. For example:

"One uses stone, wood, cement, and turns them into houses or palaces; that's construction. It calls for skill.

"But, suddenly, you touch my heart; you make me feel good. I am happy. I say: it's beautiful. This is architecture. It is art.

"If my house works well, I am grateful, as I would be to the railroads and the telephone company. But my heart has not been touched. However, if the walls, rising up against the sky, affect my feelings, I become aware of your intentions. You were gentle, harsh, charming, or dignified. Your stones tell me so. Riveted to the spot, I open my eyes. My eyes see something that conveys an idea—an idea expressed, not in words or sounds, but solely through prismatic forms, shapes clearly defined by light, which are related to each other. These relationships have nothing to do with practical functions or descriptive effects. They are a mathematical creation of the mind. They are the language of architecture. You not only have adapted raw materials to the functional requirements of a project but also, *transcending* these requirements, have established relationships that stir my emotions. That is architecture." (3, p. 123)

"Of course, if the roof leaks, if the heating system fails, if the walls crack, the delights of architecture are greatly impaired; it is as though a gentleman listening to a symphony were sitting on a pincushion or in a draft." (3, p. 175)

Le Corbusier explains these emotions as follows:

"The purpose of engineering is TO CREATE STRUCTURES; the purpose of architecture is TO CREATE EMOTIONS. Architectural emotion arises when a work strikes a chord within us that harmonizes with universal laws we recognize, submit to, and admire. When certain proportions are established, the work takes hold of us. Architecture is proportion—a pure creation of the mind." (3, p. 9)

"Architecture, which deals with plastic experiences, must, in its own realm, BEGIN AT THE BEGINNING and USE SUCH ELEMENTS AS ARE CAPABLE OF ACTING ON OUR SENSES, OF SATISFYING OUR VISUAL NEEDS, and so arrange them THAT THEIR VISUAL IMPACT—delicacy or brutality, turmoil or serenity, indifference or concern—IS CLEAR. These are plastic elements, forms that are clearly visible to our eyes and that we can measure with our minds. Such forms, which may be elementary or subtle, smooth or rough, work physiologically upon our senses (sphere, cube, cylinder, horizontal, vertical, oblique, etc.) and stimulate them. When thus affected, we are able to see beyond bare sensations; certain relationships are born that, acting upon our consciousness, lift us into a state of delight (or harmony with the universal laws that govern us and all our actions) in which we can use our full powers of recollection, reason, and creation." (3, p. 7)

This theme, set forth in the first chapter of his first book on architecture, holds an important place in all of Le Corbusier's works. It can be summed up in a single word: HARMONY. Harmony is the topic of a separate chapter, but at this point, the general meaning of the word needs clarification:

"What mechanism will trigger this high *'delight'*? *Harmony*. What a vague-sounding word!

"Nonetheless the phenomenon is simple: to precisely relate finite quantities.

"*Proportions.* Are we sufficiently aware that it's all here, that our capacity to perceive proportions, and this alone, determines our spiritual values? We are surrounded by proportions of all kinds: in nature, in human constructions, in events—multiple, countless series of proportions. . . .

"The mechanism of proportions cannot operate effectively unless the quantities it regulates are comprehensible, legible.

"This is where geometry intervenes, geometry's wonderful symbols of clarity, meaning, and spiritual structure in the midst of our muddled vision of nature." (8, p. 3)

"We say a face is beautiful when the precision of its modeling and the disposition of its features reveal proportions we find *harmonious*—harmonious because, deep down, beyond the range of our senses, they produce a resonance, a sort of sounding board that begins to vibrate: a sign of some indefinable absolute operating in the depths of our being.

"This sounding board, vibrating in us, is our criterion of harmony. Man must be built upon this axis, in perfect agreement with nature and, probably, the universe—the same organizing axis that seems to underlie all natural phenomena and objects. This axis points to some unifying principle in the universe and a single, original intent.

"The laws of physics seem to stem from this axis; we recognize (and love) science and its creations because we sense they are determined by this original intent." (3, p. 165)

Le Corbusier then formulates a "possible definition of harmony":

". . . a moment of congruence with the axis that lies within us and therefore with the laws governing the universe, a return to an underlying order. This could explain why the appearance of certain objects gives us a sense of satisfaction—a satisfaction experienced, time and again, by everyone." (3, p. 171)

Le Corbusier has said that "architecture is the skillful, correct, and magnificent play of volumes assembled in light." He also stressed the importance of proportion, by which he meant the relationship of each dimension to the total volume:

"Architecture is more than orderly arrangements or beautiful prismatic forms in light. There is something in it that transports us: this is proportion. To set in proportion is to divide into rhythmic quantities animated by the same spirit, to make this subtle, unifying proportion flow through all parts, to form an equilibrium, *to solve the equation*." (3, p. 130)

Proportion is an essential principle of architecture:

"Architectural sensations are produced by the way we perceive distances, dimensions, heights, and volumes. This mathematics provides a key that, if properly used, makes for unity. Yet, strangely enough, this key, *proportion*, has been lost, forgotten: all-important in certain epochs, leading even to sacred mysteries, it is no longer something we think or care about. We have abandoned it. Such is our present state." (20, § 9)

Another element of architectural emotion is the perception of an *intention*:

"The evolution of my reasoning, through which I hope to make you see architecture, leads me to the following summit: *intention*. The concrete or abstract elements of architecture must be governed by an intention. You have to select the proper techniques, choose materials, fulfill a program, etc., but the end result of all these efforts hinges solely on the quality of the intention." (20, § 15)

And again:

"Architecture is an irrefutable event. It occurs in certain moments of creation when the mind, preoccupied with the strength and practical convenience of a work, is suddenly uplifted by a higher intention . . . and sets out to express the lyric powers that animate and delight us. . . . This higher intention defines architecture." (8, p. 1)

In a chapter called "Greatness Is in the Mind," Le Corbusier uses the following anecdote to clarify his idea of "intention":

"As we cross the frontier between France and Belgium, the train passes through coal-mining country. What is this—a mirage? As far as the eye can see, gigantic pyramids rising from the plain stand out against the sky. I am speaking of my first trip, a long time ago. I was intensely moved. These sublime monuments thrust themselves into the blue depths on either side of the train. Yet they were merely slag heaps, those piles of gray black shale in which the veins of coal had been embedded. Then I understood: the tracks set on the side of each slope carry the tip trucks to the top of the pyramids, where they unload. The law governing the angle of repose has, once and for all, shaped the destiny of these pyramids: a perfect slope of forty-five degrees. Am I near Cairo, the land of the Pharaohs?

"Not at all! My emotion, though still sharp, is blunted. My admiration dissolves. These are not works of art; these are not works of any kind. They are simple piles of discarded shale. And all of a sudden I am aware of the gaping abyss between the appearance of an object and the quality of the mind that produced it. Intention is what moves us most deeply: the quality of mind brought to the creation of a work. But this is merely an industrial enterprise, devoid of any high intention. However fresh my judgment, however innocent my heart, I do not hear the words of a man or men. I see merely a fact, a physical law. The only remaining emotion lies in the rigor of this law. Nothing more.

"But a question arises in my mind: what if men had done this deliberately, to lift our hearts with an intention? . . .

"Our hearts appeal to other hearts. This is the measure of our emotion. Mere size can often be depressing, and the shale pyramid can make us sad. Greatness lies in the intention, not the size." (13, p. 33)

But he warns us:

"Since the mind likes to argue, to decipher an intention, to understand the game it has been invited to play, nothing repels it more than 'obvious solutions.' Art is made of subtleties, and the mind can explore these subtleties forever. Even when it finally feels satisfied, it suddenly discovers new intentions in the work it had so long been contemplating." (8, p. 10)

Reiterating his all-important distinction between architecture and engineering, Le Corbusier warns us that what is useful is not necessarily beautiful:

"Today's most gifted young people tend to reject the very word *esthetics*. They try to purify their work by limiting themselves to an austere study of useful functions; that's how we revert to the empty verbalism that has deluded many other generations: *The useful is beautiful.* What hollow reasoning!"

And he explains:

". . . If reason held uncontested sway, our lives would be governed by an exact correlation of cause and effect that would long since have extinguished humanity. In fact, we are driven by passions. Each by his own. It is often difficult to fuse what is irresistible in passion with what is incontestable in reason. These two elements enter into the chemistry of any work, but in very different proportions. Sometimes they combine to produce a strange, unexpected, breathtaking, overpowering effect, which compels our approval, excites our applause, and unites us in common admiration; this is a work of art composed of the same elements that everyone uses but that, under certain happy circumstances, are so combined as to excite us, touch us, and elicit universal acclaim.

"Esthetics thus contains a factor that makes a work immortal and ensures that there will always be immortal works. *That factor is the individual.*" (8, p. 147)

To sum it up:

"Art is poetry: a sensual emotion, the intellectual delight of appraising and judging. It is recognition of a central principle that affects our innermost being. Art is that pure creation of the mind that, at certain times, shows us the summit of *creations* man can attain. And it makes us intensely happy *to feel that we are creating.*" (3, p. 181)

CHAPTER II
How to Design Architecture

Le CORBUSIER'S WRITINGS not only describe the goals of architecture but also explain how to reach these goals. His definition of architecture covers all aspects of the profession:

"We have seen that to build a house is to erect posts, set up partitions, make openings in facades; and, inside, to arrange consecutive spaces that will work on us, that will affect us as powerfully as a lofty peak or the infinity of the sea. And we have seen that this would allow us to establish exceptionally eloquent proportions. We even went so far as to say that we were bound to create such proportions because this, fundamentally, is architecture. And that our professional responsibility to our clients—since this entails no additional expense but depends solely on the miracle of mind—requires us to make the house where they will live give its maximum yield; in other words, it requires that we offer them the high delight of architecture." (8, p. 66)

How can an architect meet these demands? In a lecture at the School of Exact Sciences in Buenos Aires, delivered in 1929, Le Corbusier described the step-by-step process of architectural design. The first step is the arrangement of volumes or, in Le Corbusier's terminology, the "characters":

"I am going to show you how architectural sensations are produced: by our reaction to geometric forms.

Fig. 1   Fig. 2

Fig. 3

"I draw an elongated prism (Fig. 1), then a cube (Fig. 2).

"This, I tell you, is the definitive, the fundamental, principle of architectural sensation. The shock has occurred. In setting this prism, with its proportions, into space, you are saying: *This is who I am.*

"You feel it more clearly when the cubic prism grows thinner and rises and the elongated prism grows flatter and stretches out (Fig. 3). You are confronting *characters*; you have created characters.

"And no matter what you may add to the work, in the way of delicacy or sturdiness, contortion or clarity, everything is now determined; you will no longer be able to modify the original sensation.

"It is worth taking the time to let this profound truth sink in. Before our pencil draws . . . . anything we may like in the style of any epoch, let us repeat to ourselves: *'I have determined my work.'* Let us therefore verify, meditate, appraise, and define before proceeding any further."

The second step is the determination of the proportions of facades:

"And here is how architectural sensations continue to act incisively upon our minds and hearts:

"I draw a door, a window, and still another window (Fig. 4).

"What has happened? I had to make doors and windows; it was my duty to do so, my practical problem. But what has happened architecturally? We have created geometric figures; we have posed the terms of an equation. So

24

Plate 1: The Senate on the Capitol in Rome.

Plate 2: Villa at Garches, 1927. Front view.

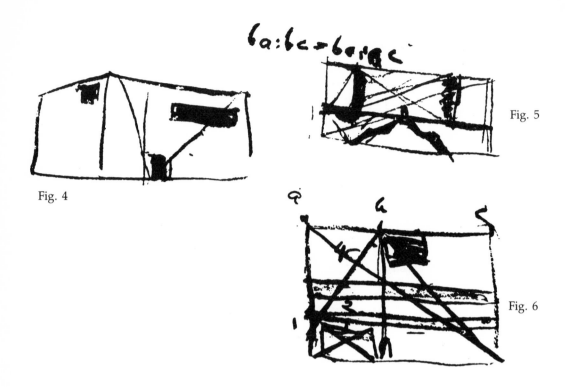

Fig. 4

Fig. 5

Fig. 6

now watch out! Suppose our equation is incorrect, insoluble? I mean to say suppose we have placed our doors and our windows so badly that there is no *truth*—no mathematical truth—in the relationship between these holes and the resulting sufaces between the holes?

"Consider Michelangelo's *Capitol** in Rome (Fig. 5). The first sensation is cubic; then comes a second sensation: the two wings, the center, and the stairs. Now see how *these different elements are governed by an underlying harmony,* which is to say kinship, unity. Not uniformity; on the contrary, contrast within a mathematical unity. This is why the *Capitol* is a masterpiece.

"I developed a real passion for playing with these basic elements of architectural sensation. Look at the diagram showing the proportions of the Villa at Garches (Fig. 6). *Inventing proportions,* choosing the location and size of openings, establishing the height in relation to a width determined by the nature of the site, these are all part of the act of creation: the kind of work produced, from a deep reserve of acquired knowledge and experience, by the creative power of the individual." (9, p. 71)

Le Corbusier continues, explaining how he determined the proportions of this villa:

*The facade of the Senate on the Capitol.

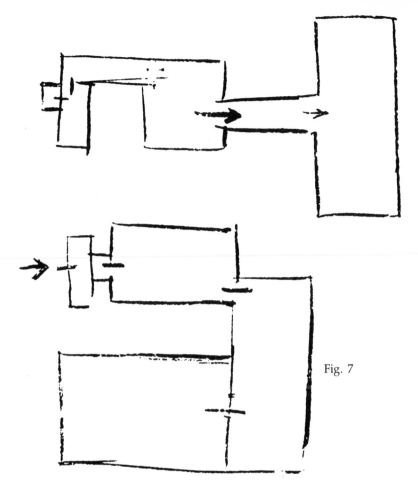

Fig. 7

"But the mind, always curious and eager, wants to look into the heart of that crude product where the destiny of the work is already, once and for all, inscribed. Its readings, and the adjustments resulting from these readings, give the following result: a mathematical (arithmetic or geometric) rectification based on the Golden Section,* on the interplay of the perpendicular diagonals, and on a 1, 2, 4 arithmetic relation between the string courses, etc. All the parts of this facade are thereby harmonized. Precision has created something definitive, sharp, true, inalterable, and permanent, which is the *architectural moment*. This architectural moment tells us what to see and how to think; it dominates, subjugates, imposes itself on us. Such is the language of architecture. To create an arresting work that powerfully imposes itself on space, I first need a perfectly shaped surface. I must then enhance the flatness of this surface with a few projections or openings that will introduce an in-and-out motion, then locate the windows (window openings play an essential role in our reading of architectural works). The placing of windows produces an

---

*Le Corbusier's use of regulating diagrams is treated in chapter IV. Here, it suffices to indicate that the formula $ba \div bc = bc \div ac$, noted on his sketch (Fig. 6), is an arithmetic expression of the Golden Section. For a more detailed discussion of the villa at Garches see p.61

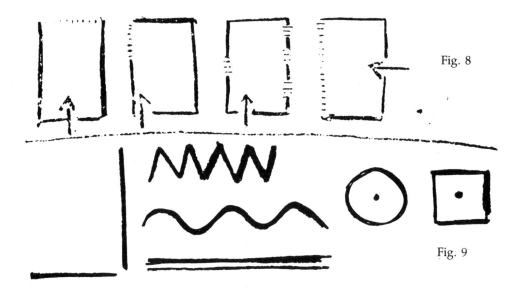

Fig. 8

Fig. 9

impressive interplay of secondary surfaces, which introduces architectural rhythms, distances, intervals." (9, p. 73)

The same interplay of volumes, surfaces, and openings occurs in the interior of a house:

"An architect is, professionally, honor bound to show the utmost solicitude for the interior of a house. On entering, we register a shock; this is the first sensation. We are impressed by a room of a certain size leading on to a room of another size, by a room of a certain shape leading on to a room of a different shape. This is what architecture is!

"And the way you enter a room, which is to say the way the door is placed in the wall, will determine the kind of shock you will receive. This is what architecture is (Fig. 7)!

"But what gives you this architectural shock? The impact of the proportions that you see. What produces these proportions? The objects or surfaces you see, because they are *in the light*. The human animal is strongly affected by sunlight: this response is rooted in the inmost nature of the species.

"Consider, then, the supreme importance of placing windows; see how the walls of the room are affected by the light (Fig. 8). This, in effect, is a crucial moment in architectural design, a source of decisive architectural

Plate 3: The Parthenon

impressions. You can easily see that styles and decors no longer count. Think of those early spring days when the sky is full of wind-swept clouds; you are in your house; a cloud hides the sky: how sad you feel! The wind chases the cloud away; the sun comes through the window: how happy you feel! Other clouds plunge you back into shade: how eagerly you think of approaching summer, which will give you constant light!" (9, p. 74)

He ends by describing the sensations produced by forms, rhythms, light:

"Light and forms, specific intensities of light, successive spaces—these all act on our sensibility, producing physiological sensations that scholars have recorded, described, classified, and specified. This horizontal and this vertical, this harshly serrated line or this gentle undulation, the closed and centered form of a circle or a square—these all work strongly on us, characterize our creations, and determine our sensations (Fig. 9). Rhythm, variety or monotony, coherence or incoherence, a surprise that may enchant or disappoint us, joy of light or chill of darkness, the serenity of a sunny room or the anguish of a room filled with dark corners, elation or depression, these are all consequences of the things I have been drawing, and they act on our sensibility through a series of irresistible impressions."

To sum up:

"Once you are aware of the all-powerful eloquence of lines, your minds will no longer be encumbered by petty decorative events and, more important, your future architectural creations will be based on the right chronology, a *hierarchy* that gives first place to essentials. You will realize that these architectural essentials depend on the quality of your choice, on the vigor of your mind, and not on rich materials, marbles, rare woods, or ornaments, which are useful only as a last resort—meaning, in effect, that they are not very useful at all." (9, p. 74)

Le Corbusier here explains what he calls "the center of all measurements," a right angle formed by a horizontal and a vertical:

"I should like to teach you to feel something that is sublime, something through which the human mind, at the high points of civilization, has shown its mastery; I call it *'the center of all measurements.'* Look at this:

"I am in Brittany; this pure line is the horizon of the ocean; a vast horizontal plane stretches toward me (Fig. 10). I take a sensual delight in the majestic stillness. There are some rocks on the right. I am enchanted by the sinuous lines of the sandy beaches, which are like a very gentle modulation of the horizontal plane. I was walking. I stop suddenly. A sensational event has occurred between the horizon and my eyes: a vertical rock, a granite stone, is standing there, like a menhir; this vertical and the horizon of the sea form a right angle. The site has been crystallized, fixed. This is a place where we stop because we are in the presence of a magnificent and total symphony of proportions, of nobility. The vertical fixes the meaning of the horizontal. Each line lives by the other. The full power of a synthesis is made manifest.

"I ponder. Why am I so deeply moved? Why have I sometimes experienced the same emotion in other circumstances and under other forms?

"The Parthenon comes to mind, the overwhelming power of its sublime

Fig. 10

ITEM ON HOLD

Ideas of Le Corbusier on architecture and urban planning / texts edited and presented by Jacques Guiton ; translation by Margaret Guiton.
Le Corbusier, 1887-1965.
720.944 J34ID

Fig. 12

Fig. 13

"the center of all measurements"

31

Plate 4: The Tour de Beurre—Rouen Cathedral

entablature (Fig. 11). I consider, by way of contrast, of comparison, certain works that are very sensitive but somehow aborted, unrealized: the Tour de Beurre in Rouen (Fig. 12), for example, the flamboyant arches on which so much delicate genius was spent without attaining the brilliance, the brazen trumpet-voiced brilliance, of the Parthenon on the Acropolis.

"So I draw, in two lines, this 'center of all measurements,' and after mentally comparing many human works with one another, I tell myself: 'Here it is; it is sufficient' " (Fig. 13). (9, p. 76)

Le Corbusier then shows how a building interacts with its surroundings:

"I am now on the trail of broader architectural concepts. I see that the structure we are erecting is neither alone nor isolated, that the surrounding atmosphere constitutes other partitions, floors, and ceilings, and that the harmony that brought me to a sudden halt before the rock in Brittany exists— can exist—everywhere and at all times. The structure is no longer self-contained: the outdoors exists. The outdoors envelops me in its totality, like a room. Harmony finds its sources far away, everywhere, in all things. How far removed we are from 'styles' and pretty drawings on paper!

"I am going to show you the same house—this simple rectangular prism.

"We are on a plain, a flat plain. Do you see how the site collaborates with me (Fig. 14)?

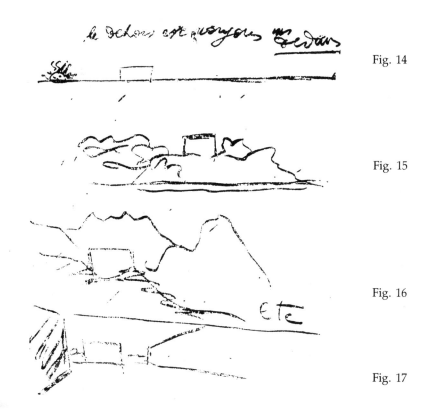

Fig. 14

Fig. 15

Fig. 16

Fig. 17

"We are on the wooded hillsides of Tourraine. The same house is different (Fig. 15).

"Here it is, defying the savage profiles of the Alps (Fig. 16).

"Our sensibility, in each case, discovers different marvels.

"The latent qualities of the surrounding atmosphere, which influence the character of a building, are immediate realities for those able to see and use them.

"Here is the same house—this rectangular prism—at a street crossing, submitting to the pressure of the surrounding buildings (Fig. 17).

"Here it is at the end of an avenue lined with poplars, assuming a somewhat ceremonial air (Fig. 18).

"Here it is at the end of an empty road, supported by groves on either side (Fig. 19).

"And here it is, finally, jumping right out at us unexpectedly as we reach the end of a street. If a man walks by, his gestures, intimately tied to the 'human scale' of the facade, will stand out clearly and legibly against it like those of an actor on the stage (Fig. 20)." (9, p. 78)

According to Le Corbusier, simplicity is a basic principle of architectural design:

"Our *search for architecture* has led to the discovery of simplicity. Great

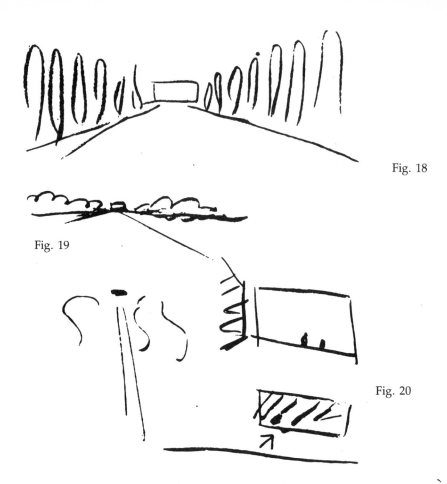

Fig. 18

Fig. 19

Fig. 20

art—we must never tire of repeating this—is produced by simple means. History shows that the mind tends toward simplicity. Simplicity, which results from judgments and choices, is a sign of mastery. It gives, through a clearly perceptible play of forms, the means of expressing a state of mind, of revealing a spiritual system. It is like an *affirmation*, a path leading from confusion to clear geometric statements. At the dawn of modern times, when, after the Middle Ages, peoples stabilized their social or political systems, a newfound serenity stimulated their appetite for spiritual clarity. The great Renaissance cornice wants to delineate sharply against the sky the system of proportions that is resting on the ground (Fig. 21); the equivocal, oblique form of the pitched roof has been repudiated (Fig. 22). The seventeenth and eighteenth centuries and the Napoleonic era show a growing determination to express clearly 'the center of proportions' " (Fig. 23).

Le Corbusier also gives a modern example, flat-roofed buildings standing on stilts:

"Reinforced concrete has brought flat roofs (Fig. 24) with interior drain pipes and many other structural innovations. It is no longer really possible to draw a cornice, for this is no longer a living architectural entity; the function of the cornice no longer exists. But we have found the sharp, pure line that a flat-roofed building cuts across a brilliant sky.

In search of the simple, but simplicity is not poverty; it is a distillation.

"New techniques have also produced a useful instrument for those who create plastic forms: stilts. What a marvelous way to lift the *center of proportions,* the *center of all measurements,* into the air, where its four sides are plainly visible! Thanks to reinforced concrete or steel, this raised prism is more legible than ever before (Fig. 25).

"*So, simplicity is not equivalent to poverty*; it is a choice, a discrimination, a crystallization. Its object is purity. Simplicity synthesizes. A ragged agglomeration of cubes is an accidental event, but a synthesis is an intellectual act." (9, p. 81)

Le Corbusier repeatedly advised architects to avoid arbitrarily complicated forms:

"Some architects have distorted minds. They have come to prefer irregular sites, in the belief that these will help them discover original solutions. These architects are mistaken." (6, p. 166)

"We have become willing to live in *arbitrary* surroundings. A fashion has grafted itself onto our sickness: the fashion of complicated forms, a taste for complicated forms. Even when we build a house in the flat countryside, we succumb to the lure of the arbitrary." (8, p. 6)

At the end of his lecture, Le Corbusier explains why, in a city, the silhouette of each building should be simple:

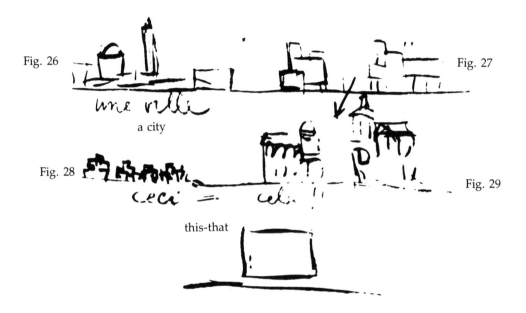

Fig. 26

a city

Fig. 27

Fig. 28

this-that

Fig. 29

"Let me say one more word about disciplining impulses that, although often very imaginative, are like the uncontrolled lashing of a colt. I am drawing the outline of a beautiful city remembered from my student travels (Fig. 26). Here is the belfry or campanile; here is the podesta's square palace. I have expressed *the silhouette of a city.* What lack of restraint and foresight we show when, as is currently fashionable, we let the silhouette of a house look like the silhouette of a city (Fig. 27)! If I increase the number of these wretched houses, in a street or a city, the effect will be disastrous: turmoil, jagged edges, cacophony (Fig. 28).

"These undisciplined good intentions produce the kind of streets you see all around you in Buenos Aires or, for that matter, in European cities—those atrocious displays of platitude, laziness, and academic pretension" (Fig. 29).

This leads to one of Le Corbusier's basic principles of city planning:

"Let us keep this diversity, so indispensable to the mind, for the day we start working on the symphony of the city. The enormous problems of con-temporary urban planning and architecture will give the city a new scale in breadth and height. The unity will lie in the details; the clamor, in the overall effect." (9, p. 83)

In *Vers une architecture,* Le Corbusier analyzed three basic elements of archi-tectural design: volumes, surfaces, and plans. He writes:

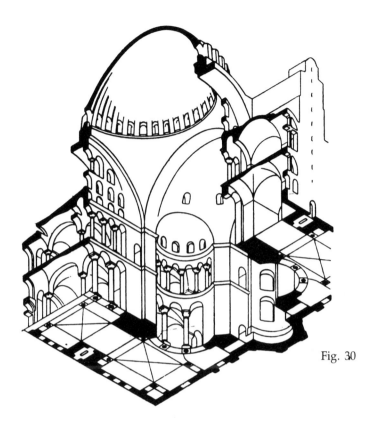

Fig. 30

"Volumes and surfaces are the elements through which architecture is made visible. Volumes and surfaces are determined by the plan. The plan is the generator. So much the worse for those who lack imagination!" (3, p. 16)

Volumes

"Architecture is the skillful, exact, and magnificent play of volumes assembled in light. Our eyes are designed to see forms in light; shadow and light reveal forms; cubes, cones, spheres, cylinders, and pyramids are the great primary forms so well revealed by light; their image is exact and tangible, free of all ambiguities. This is why they are *beautiful, the most beautiful, forms.* Everyone agrees on this point, children, primitives, and metaphysicians. It is a prerequisite of plastic art." (3, p. 16)

Surfaces

"Since architecture is the skillful, exact, and magnificent play of volumes assembled in light, the architect must bring the surfaces that envelop these volumes to life without letting them become parasites that devour the volumes by assimilating them to their own ends, as has been the sad story of present times.

"If we are to let a volume retain the splendor of its form in light but at the same time adapt the surface to functional tasks, we shall have to find, in the necessary subdivisions of the surfaces, such elements as will *accentuate, generate,* the form. In other words, an architectural work may be a house, a temple, or a factory. The surface of a temple or a factory is generally a wall pierced with doors and windows; these openings, which often destroy the form, must be made to accentuate the form. Since architecture consists fundamentally of spheres, cones, and cylinders, the elements that generate and accentuate these forms will be based on pure geometry." (3, p. 25)

Plans

"The plan is the generator.

"The spectator's eye moves through a site made of streets and houses. It registers the shock of the volumes that rise up around it. If these volumes are forms that have not been debased by inappropriate alterations, if their grouping expresses a clear rhythm, not an incoherent cacophony, if the proportions between the volumes and the intervening spaces are correct, the eye will transmit to the brain coordinated sensations that are intensely pleasing to the mind: this is architecture.

"Inside,* the eye perceives the multiple surfaces of walls and vaults. The cupolas determine spaces; the vaults unfold surfaces; the columns and the walls interact intelligibly with one another. The whole structure rises from its base and follows a rule that is inscribed on the ground, in the plan: beautiful forms, many varieties of forms, a unifying geometric principle. A profound sense of harmony prevails: this is architecture.

"The plan is basic. Where there is no plan, there is no greatness of intention and expression, no rhythm, no volume, no coherence. Where there is no plan, we experience that sensation of formlessness, indigence, disorder, unreason, that the human mind cannot endure.

"The plan calls for a highly active imagination. It also calls for severe self-discipline. The plan determines everything else; it is the decisive moment!" (3, p. 35)

However, as Le Corbusier here implies, we must never forget that this two-dimensional plan, which can be read in a single glance, describes three-dimensional volumes that will be seen successively:

"Architecture can be seen only *by a walking man* . . . so much so that when it comes to the test, buildings can be classified as alive or dead according to whether the rule *of movement* has been applied or not. (20, §4)

"As Arab architecture shows, we cannot understand the development of an architectural composition unless we are walking, moving from one place to another.

". . . This house [the Villa Savoye] is a real architectural walk that offers a series of constantly varied, unexpected, sometimes astonishing views."**

Le Corbusier also examines a fourth element of architectural design that he calls "MODÉNATURE." The term, which has no exact equivalent, might be

---

*Le Corbusier is referring to the interior of Santa Sophia in Istanbul (Fig. 30). (Sketch from *Histoire de l'architecture* by Auguste Choisy)

**Le Corbusier and Pierre Jeanneret—*Oeuvre complète de 1929–1934*, p. 24, Willy Boesiger, Zurich: Girsberger, 1935, and Artemis.

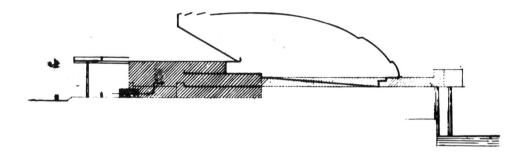

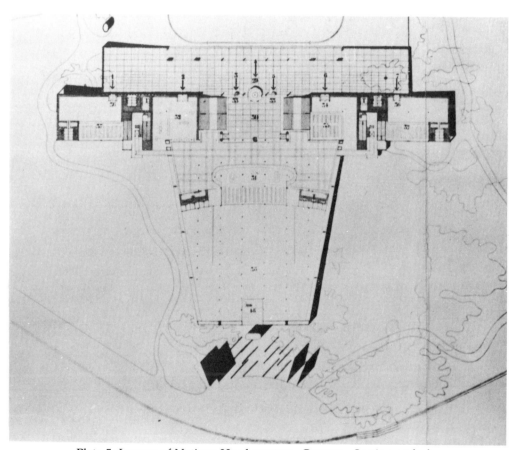

Plate 5: League of Nations Headquarters, Geneva—Section and plan.

Plate 6: Swiss Pavilion, Paris.

Plate 7: Cook house, Boulogne-sur-Seine.

translated as "delineation." In the following explanation I shall use the French word and let Le Corbusier define its meaning:

" 'Modénature' is not the same thing as the design of moldings, which is well known . . . and often done. The word *modénature* can be applied to a building without cornices or moldings: it refers to the profile, everything that determines the profile, in the same way that it would refer to the profile of a man with a turned-up or hooked nose, a flat or rounded forehead, etc.

". . . The word *modénature* is no longer used today because the thing itself has disappeared: consider the Gare d'Orsay, the Grand Palais! But the word comes to mind again because our new methods of construction (without stones) force us to seek an appropriate esthetic; the taut and inalienable character of an architectural work, in effect its *face*, its inner spirit, is solely given and determined by the proportions of its profile, by the 'modénature.' " (7, p. 117)

Le Corbusier stresses this concept:

"The plan of a house, its volume and surfaces, is determined in part by the practical requirements of the problem and in part by the imagination, the act of plastic creation. In his plan, and consequently in everything that arises from the plan, the architect is already creating plastic forms; he is subjecting practical requirements to the plastic goal he is pursuing: *he is designing.*

Plate 8: Villa Savoye, Poissy.

"He must then delineate *the features of the face,* using the interplay of light and shade to help express his meaning. *This is 'modénature.'* And 'modénature' is free of all constraint; it is a purely inventive process that either brightens or dims a face. 'Modénature' reveals the plastic artist; the engineer retreats; the sculptor sets to work. 'Modénature' is the acid test of the architect; it leaves him no alternative: to be or not to be a plastic artist." (3, p. 177)

"Modénature," as a pure creation of the mind, is a highly personal process. In making this point, Le Corbusier again returns to the Greek masterpiece he so admired—The Parthenon:

"Greece, and in Greece the Parthenon, marks the summit of this pure creation of the mind: 'modénature.'

"Since this is a purely inventive process, it must necessarily proceed from an individual mind. Phidias created the Parthenon, for Ictinos and Callicrates, the official architects of the Parthenon, built other Doric temples that seem cold and rather flat. Passion, generosity, nobility, are inscribed in the geometries of its 'modénature'—quantities arranged in exact proportions. Phidias, the great sculptor Phidias, built the Parthenon.

"No other architectural work, anywhere, of any period, can equal it. At that crucial moment of history, a man stirred by the noblest thoughts crystallized them in a sculpture of light and shade. The 'modénature' of the Parthenon is infallible, implacable. Its rigor transcends our normal habits and possibilities. Here stands the purest testimony to the physiology of sensation and to the mathematical speculation that supports it; we are transported by its sensuality, ravished by its intelligence; we reach the axis of harmony. The question of religious dogma, symbolic description, and naturalistic representation no longer arises: these are pure forms in exact proportions and nothing else.

"For 2,000 years those who have seen the Parthenon have realized that it constitutes a decisive moment in architecture." (3, p. 179)

Le Corbusier, using his own works as examples—the League of Nations Headquarters project in Geneva (Plate 5), the Swiss Pavilion at the Cité Universitaire in Paris (Plate 6), the Cook house at Boulogne-sur-Seine (Plate 7), and the Villa Savoye at Poissy (Plate 8)—sums up his ideas on architecture as follows:

"The section of a building [Plate 5, top] contains its essential spirit: the destiny of the volumes is determined by incisive lines, as it were, engraved in steel.

"The plan of a building [Plate 5, bottom] is a human appropriation of space. We walk about the plan; our eyes look forward, for perception is sequential; it takes place in time; it is a series of visual events, just as a symphony is a series of auditory events. Time, duration, sequence, and continuity are the constituent elements of architecture. . . .

"Architecture, through the plan and the section, is closely akin to music."

And finally:

"We are here [Plates 6, 7, 8] immersed in the full music of forms. Each one is there to play with those that surround it. Whether a palace or a house, each is governed by a similar intention: the intention (once all practical problems have been resolved—construction, function, cost) of smiling, of speaking clearly. . . . This entails no additional expense beyond an expenditure of imaginative energy. . . . Once we have drawn up the plan and the section, the game has started. But there are also structure and skin, weights, loads, and bearing members. There is the unity of the whole, the sculptural gamble, the temerity of the construction, the challenge! There are acrobatics, sport, wit. We are enjoying ourselves; yes, we have had a wonderful time risking everything. It was a perilous game. Without danger, life, like everything else, is devoid of tension, interest, sun, storms, thunderbolts, or relief."*

---

*L'Architecture d'aujourd'hui, numéro spécial, p. 44, 1948.

CHAPTER III
Some Examples

T HIS CHAPTER gives an idea of Le Corbusier's approach to architectural design by quoting certain passages of his writings that describe the architectural conception of his buildings and show how fortuitous events or accidents sometimes influenced his design. But first: how did Le Corbusier attack a new problem?

"When given an assignment, I have a habit of committing it *to memory* by not allowing myself to make any sketches for several months. The human mind is, by nature, fairly autonomous. It is a container into which we can pour the elements of a problem helter-skelter and let them float, simmer, and ferment for a while. Then, one day, a spontaneous inner impulse triggers a reaction. We pick up a pencil, a piece of charcoal, or a colored pencil (color is the key to this process) and put it down on paper. The idea, or child, emerges. It has come into the world; *it has been born.*" (35, p. 1)

Le Corbusier has explained how he designed the chapel at Ronchamp. A determining factor was the presence, on this inaccessible hilltop, of stones from the earlier chapel destroyed during the war. Though damaged, they were still usable:

"June 1950, on the hill: I spend three hours familiarizing myself with the site and the horizons, letting it all sink in. The chapel, torn open by shells, is still

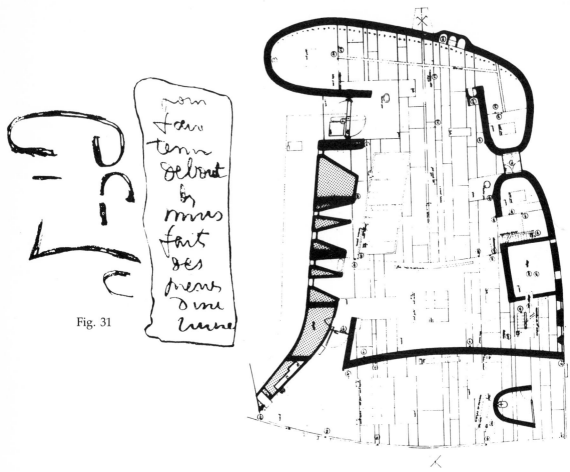

Fig. 31

standing. The committee, the priest, and some local contractors stand by while I investigate the situation. Since there is no road that will permit trucks to carry the usual building materials up to the hill, I shall make do with sand and cement. The stones of the demolished chapel, which are somewhat porous and calcined, cannot be used for bearing walls but will serve for filling. An idea emerges.

"Under such conditions, at the top of this isolated hill, *there should be only one trade**: a homogenous, skilled team of workers—men apart, free men in charge of their own work. Good luck!" (33, p. 88)

Le Corbusier was also inspired by the site:

"An idea in search of itself wanders around my mind. While I was on the hill, I had carefully drawn the four horizons. For there are four: in the east, the Ballons d'Alsace; on the south, the last foothills rising from a valley; in the west, the plain of the Saône; in the north, a valley and a village. These drawings, which have been mislaid or lost, trigger the architectural response—*a visual echo of the landscape . . .*" (33, p. 89)

The poor quality of the stones Le Corbusier had decided to use as filling none-theless accounts for the unusual layout of the walls: curved or hooked shapes

---

*The masons who, in small French towns, do several different kinds of work: mansory, cement, reinforced concrete, forms, etc.

46

Plate 9: The chapel of Ronchamp during construction.

Plate 10: The chapel of Ronchamp completed.

Plate 11: Chapel of Ronchamp—Inside view looking east.

that would ensure stability. In a note appended to a sketch of the plan he explains:

"So that walls made from the stones of a ruin will stand up." (Fig. 31)

Le Corbusier describes the structural system of the chapel as follows:

"On my drafting board I have a crab shell that I picked up on Long Island in 1946. It will become the chapel roof: two membranes of reinforced concrete six centimeters (2½ in.) thick and 2.26 meters (7 ft. 5 in.) apart. . . ." (33, p. 90)

"The shell is placed over the deliberately heavy walls in which reinforced concrete columns have been embedded. The shell will rest, here and there, on top of these columns, but it will not touch the walls; the ten-centimeter-wide (4 in.) horizontal ray of light that penetrates will create an astonishing effect. . . ." (33, p. 95)

Le Corbusier then explains the construction of the south wall with its glazed openings. His first sketches show that he intended to use stone masonry in this section as well but later changed the design, turning the wall into a real three-dimensional sculpture, which is especially striking when seen from inside.

"A few vertical, triangular-shaped slabs of reinforced concrete, 16 centimeters (6¼ in.) thick, ranging from a width of 3.70 meters (12 ft.) to one of 1.40 meters (4 ft. 7 in.) at the base and narrowing to 50 centimeters (1 ft. 8 in.) at the top, carry the huge overhanging shell of the roof. The surface of the wall—in-

Plate 12: Chapel of Ronchamp—Inside view looking south.

cluding the deep, splayed recesses for the glazed openings, wide at the interior surface of the wall and narrow on the facade—is a 4-centimeter (1¾ in.) layer of concrete sprayed with a cement gun onto a surface of expanded wire mesh." (33, p. 99)

During one of his lectures, Le Corbusier analyzed the different types of plans used in the numerous houses he built with Pierre Jeanneret:

"Architects express ideas in different ways, according to their individual temperaments. They can nonetheless observe, judge, know themselves, and act clear-sightedly. Pierre Jeanneret and I have built a good many houses. As I analyze our work, I can perceive the general intention determining the character of different buildings. Using consistent methods, regarding *priorities, dimensions, flow of traffic, layout,* and *proportions,* we have thus far used four distinct types of plan, each corresponding to a particular intellectual purpose.

"In the *first* type each element grows organically beside its neighbor. The impulse emanates from the interior and pushes against the exterior, producing various projections. This principle leads to a 'pyramidlike' design, which can become contorted if not restrained. (Auteuil) (Fig. 32)

"In the *second* type the organic parts are contained by a rigid, clean-cut en-

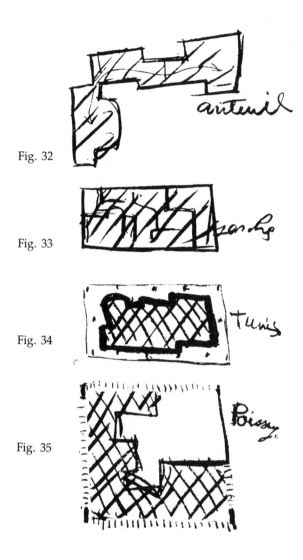

Fig. 32

Fig. 33

Fig. 34

Fig. 35

velope. This poses a challenging problem that no doubt appeals to the mind: our intellectual energies work against self-imposed limitations. (Garches) (Fig. 33)

"The *third* type, which has an exposed frame, is a simple envelope, as clear and transparent as a grille. It allows us to fit in rooms of varying shapes and sizes as needed, with a different layout on each floor. It is an ingenious type, particularly appropriate to certain climates. It is a plan that is flexible and full of possibilities. (Tunis) (Fig. 34)

"The *fourth* type has the simple external form of the second type, but its interior has the advantages and qualities of the first and third. A clear and very generous type, this, too, has many possibilities. (Poissy) (Fig. 35)

"It is helpful, I repeat, to study one's own work constantly. An awareness of one's evolution is the springboard of progress." (9, p. 134)

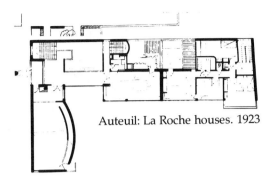

Auteuil: La Roche houses. 1923

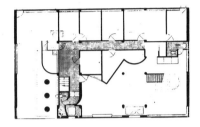

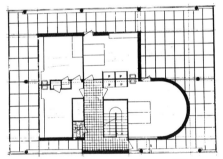

Tunis: Villa at Carthage. 1929

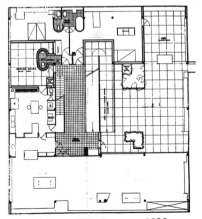

Poissy: Villa Savoye. 1928

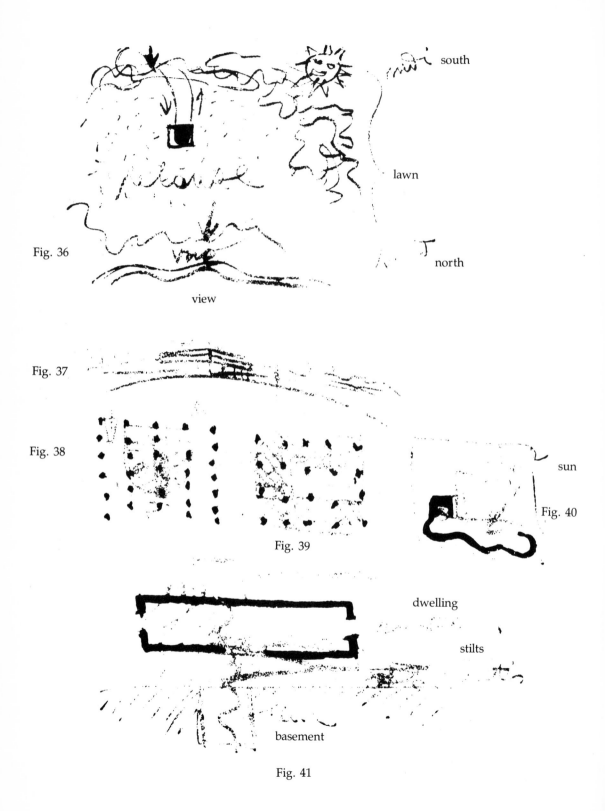

Fig. 36

south

lawn

north

view

Fig. 37

Fig. 38

Fig. 39

sun

Fig. 40

dwelling

stilts

basement

Fig. 41

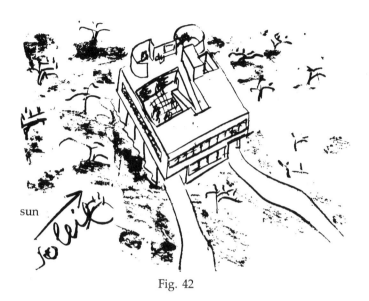

Fig. 42

Le Corbusier then examines in more detail the Villa Savoye at Poissy, his example of the type *four* plan:

"Let us, in conclusion, analyze this building now under construction at Poissy, near Paris.

"The visitors, thus far, wander around the interior, wondering what it is all about and failing to grasp the rationale of what they see and feel. They do not find any trace of what is called a house. They feel as if they were inside something else entirely new. And . . . I do not think that they are bored!

"The site is a wide lawn shaped like a flattened dome. The main view looks north. The house, if oriented toward the view, would thus face away from the sun" (Fig. 36).

Le Corbusier solved the problem by designing a building facing all directions:

"The house is a raised box segmented by a continuous strip window. This simplifies the interplay of solids and voids. The box, situated in the midst of meadowlands, overlooks an orchard (Fig. 37).

"A driveway passes under the box, between the stilts, forming, as it goes in and out, a hairpin curve around the core of the house, which includes the entrance, the hall, the garage, and the servants' quarters (bedrooms, laundry, linen closet). The cars drive under the house, where they are parked or driven out again (Fig. 38).

"A gentle ramp leads, almost imperceptibly, from the entrance hall to the main floor, where the living quarters are located: drawing room, dining room, bedrooms, etc. The continuous window on the periphery of the house provides views and sunlight for all the rooms. These surround a terrace garden, which provides and controls the sunlight. The sliding glass walls of the drawing room and several other rooms open freely onto this terrace garden: the sun thus comes in everywhere, penetrating the very center of the house (Fig. 39).

"The ramp, which is now exterior, leads from the terrace garden to the roof and the solarium (Fig. 40). In addition, a three-flight spiral staircase connects the solarium directly with the cellar dug under the ground floor. This spiral, a simple vertical organ, fits easily into the horizontal design.

"And, finally, look at the section (Fig. 41): air circulates everywhere; light reaches every point, penetrating everywhere. As one moves through the house, one sees an astonishing variety of architectural effects, disconcerting to any visitor unfamiliar with the architectural possibilities afforded by new techniques. The simple ground-floor posts, which cut the landscape at regular intervals, do away with any concept of a front or a back or a side of the house. This is a clean plan, exactly adapted to the requirements and the landscape of the Poissy countryside (Fig. 42)." (9, p. 136)

The polychrome facade of the apartment building in Marseille that le Corbusier calls a "Unité d'Habitation" illustrates the effect of an accidental event on the appearance of a building. As Le Corbusier explains, the proportions of the whole building had been based on the MODULOR scale,* thus creating a unified harmony throughout, but chance intervened:

"A sense of coherence, of proportioning, of friendly cohabitation, of the repercussion of one form on another, one surface on another, one line on another, prevails from top to bottom.

"Prevails except for two mistakes by a careless engineer, which strike a false note noticeable to any informed observer: window divisions that deviate from the correct proportions and concrete panels (between the loggias) cast on a wrong module. I was in New York at the time, immersed in the plans for the United Nations. I was so distressed by this offhand treatment of measurements in the midst of the Modulor harmonics that, in a fit of exasperation, I hit on the idea of a polychrome facade.

"But the polychromy would be so dazzling that it would wrench the mind away from the dissonances by an irresistible torrent of major color sensations.

"Had it not been for those mistakes, the Marseilles building would perhaps not have had a polychrome exterior." (30, p. 246)

The slanted facade of the Salvation Army building in Paris is a less familiar example of adaptation to an unforeseen obstacle: the authorities would not allow Le Corbusier to build the last floor, where the nursery was to be located, on the grounds that it would exceed the zoning envelope by forty centimeters (1 ft. 4 in.).

"In order to retain the nursery floor despite the zoning restriction, the architects hit on the unexpected idea of sloping the facade forty centimeters (1 ft.

---

*See chapter IV.

4 in.) inward, from the bottom to the top. The obstacle was thus bypassed. The facade slopes inward by forty centimeters (1 ft. 4 in.), and no one notices it. One can even say that this slope gives the whole building an undeniable effect of lightness."*

In the following passage, written in 1947, Le Corbusier traces the history of his investigation of ways to control the effect of sun on buildings. It is a good example of the way he studied a problem, whether of architecture or urban planning, over an extended period of time.

"It is a blissful moment when, after long efforts to coordinate different factors, you realize you have arrived at the truth—a truth that, of course, varies according to the circumstances. After twenty-five years of study a new (although basically traditional) element may perhaps be definitively incorporated into the architecture of steel, concrete, and glass. 'Brise-soleil' introduces a new technique: sun control.**

"Steel and reinforced concrete . . . led to the *open plan;* the open plan led to the *nonbearing facade;* the nonbearing facade led to *the glass skin.* It was a natural, inevitable evolution. Together with stilts, which entirely free the ground level, this evolution has created a revolution in architecture and urban design.

". . . The *glass skin* (1922), as used in houses, was freed from traditional measurements, thus providing a new scale. There followed twenty years of experimentation or, sometimes, merely proposals. The use of the glass skin (there is no progress without experimentation) revealed two disadvantages: (1) the rooms are too hot in summer in almost all latitudes; (2) in an apartment building with, for example, 2,000 residents we are faced with the delicate problem of communal window cleaning and the disorder inevitably arising out of individual treatments of the glass surface (shutters, curtains, awnings, shades, etc.).

"But it has one incontestable advantage: the glass skin replaces isolated windows. We must not abandon, we must not under any circumstances abandon, this extraordinary conquest that neither centuries nor millennia have thus far achieved.

"One day, while I was considering Mediterranean problems (1928, Carthage; 1933, Barcelona; 1930, 1933, 1938, and 1939, Algiers), my head full of these buts and ifs, the solution came to me: install, in front of the glass skin, a device regulated by the sun's daily path as it varies between the solstices and equinoxes. The 'brise-soleil,' as an architectural event, was born.

"This was in Rio de Janeiro in 1936. While working on the plans of the Ministry of National Education and Public Health with Luccio Costa, Oscar Niemeyer, Reidy, Moreiro, Carlson Lean, Vascoucelos, etc., I answered an anguished question: *Don't worry, we'll use 'brise-soleil.'* This was the reason for the anguished question: in tropical Rio facades cannot face certain directions because the sun is too strong. I drew 'brise-soleil' on a rectangular, egg crate pattern for the east and south facades and vertical 'brise-soleil' for the west facade.

---

*Le Corbusier et Pierre Jeanneret, *Oeuvre complète de* 1929–1934, p. 98. Willy Boesiger, Zurich: Girsberger, 1935, and Artémis.

**These "brise-soleil" are devices built outside of the building to reduce the heat and glare of the sun on glass surfaces. They can be made of concrete, metal, or other materials and can be either fixed or movable. In the "brise-soleil loggia," the windows are set back far enough to create an accessible balcony.

Plate 13: The *"brise-soleil"* of the Ministry of
Health and Education in Rio de Janeiro.

"The right solution had been staring me in the face for years. During my
travels I had often seen, in luxurious as well as indigenous forms of architecture,
that admirable architectural organ, the loggia. In 1939 the 'brise-soleil loggia'
was fitted into our Algiers plan. From now on one of the problems of contemporary urban design, *large apartment buildings,* can be resolved."*

Le Corbusier was delighted by the elegance of his solution. The "brise-soleil-
loggia" would not only control sunlight and glare but also replace the "little man-
sized window so well suited to three-story buildings" with a system adapted to
the scale of modern apartment buildings. It would also "brighten modern cities"
with the "smile" of its ancestor, the traditional loggia.

This illustrates an important and often unrecognized aspect of Le Corbusier's thinking: his respect for the past.

*L'Architecture d'aujourd'hui, numéro spécial, 1948, p. 48.

Plate 14: The *"brise-soleil loggia"* of the apartment building at Marseille.

"You just saw that, carried away by my defense of the right to invent, I appealed to the testimony of the past, that past which was my only master and remains my constant critic. Any thinking man, thrown into the great unknown of architectural invention, will find his sole support in the lessons of past centuries. Testimonies that have resisted time are of permanent human value. . . . Respect for the past is a filial attitude, natural in any creator, as natural as the love and respect a son feels for his father." (20, §11)

Le Corbusier, citing the examples of the Carthusian monastery of Ema, which inspired his "immeuble-villas,"* the glazed facades of Flemish buildings, and Siamese houses or lake-dwellings raised on stilts, exclaims:

"If you only knew how delighted I am to be able to say: 'My revolutionary ideas already existed at all times and in all countries.' " (9, p. 97)

---

*For a fuller account see page 89.

CHAPTER IV
Harmony: Regulating Diagrams, Golden Section, Modulor

AS WE HAVE SEEN, Le Corbusier's idea of harmony plays a major role in his theory of architectural design. This chapter describes the method he used to attain harmonious proportions: regulating diagrams,* the Golden Section, and his own MODULOR. Such methods, he points out, were used in all great periods of architecture up to and including the Renaissance, and he deplores their subsequent decline and disappearance.

It is a controversial subject. However, given Le Corbusier's passionate interest in harmony, it cannot be bypassed. He claims to have devoted his entire life to "art and, more specifically, a search for harmony," which he considers "the most beautiful of human passions." This lifelong quest led to the following conclusion:

"One feels very clearly that the precision required of any act that arouses a superior quality of emotion is based on mathematics. The result can be expressed by the single word *harmony*. Harmony is the happy coexistence of things; coexistence implies duality or multiplicity and consequently calls for proportions and consonances. What sort of consonances? Those existing between ourselves and our environment, between the spirit of man and the spirit of things, between

---

*Le Corbusier's expression *tracés régulateurs* has sometimes been translated as "regulating lines." Since it refers to a group of related lines, I thought that "regulating diagrams" approximated its meaning more closely.

mathematics as a human invention and mathematics as the secret of the universe."*

Le Corbusier's approach has frequently been ridiculed, but anyone who has felt the thoroughly satisfying and pleasing effect created by the appearance of his buildings is bound to admit that his approach has produced remarkable results. This does not seem entirely coincidental. We must also recognize that Le Corbusier's methods are widely misunderstood. Many people believe that he was talking about ready-made formulas when he was really talking about tools that, like any tools, are effective only when used effectively.

REGULATING DIAGRAMS

Le Corbusier did not conceive his TRACÉS RÉGULATEURS, or regulating diagrams, as predetermined grids on which to base designs. They were to be used only after the design had been drawn up to make the proportions more exact. He discovered a need for such diagrams at the outset of his career:

"I built my first house when I was seventeen; it was covered with decorations. I was twenty-four when I built my second house; it was white and bare: I had traveled in the meantime. The plans of this second house were lying on my drafting board. The year was 1911. I was suddenly struck by the arbitrary placing of the openings in the facade (the windows). I blacked them in with a piece of charcoal; the black spots now spoke some kind of language, but it was an incoherent language. Again I was struck by the absence of a rule or law. Appalled, I realized that I was working in utter chaos. And I then discovered, for my own purposes, the need for a regulating device. This obsession would henceforth occupy a corner of my mind."*

In a more detailed account of this discovery, Le Corbusier writes:

"I felt very clearly a need to establish some sort of a family relationship between the different elements, particularly between what the eye perceived immediately, the outline of the facade, and what it perceived next, a projecting wing, and what it perceived afterwards, the door and window openings and their surrounding wall surfaces. I needed a regulating diagram: a diagram based on diagonals, for a diagonal can express the special character of a surface in a single line. I thus drew the diagonal of the facade, that of the projecting wing, that of the door, and that of a plain surface which was an important element of the composition. I then could see that when these diagonals were parallel or perpendicular to each other, the different surfaces that they defined belonged to the same family and consequently agreed with one another. If these diagonals were not parallel or perpendicular, I did my utmost to correct them.

"But we cannot always do exactly what we want. A house is often subject to requirements that have nothing to do with geometric or plastic considerations: its height and width, for example, are often determined by zoning regulations. I was thus occasionally obliged to use two different sets of diagonals. This produced a

---

*A chapter called "Architecture and the spirit of mathematics", in a book entitled *"Les Grands courants de la pensée mathématique"*, by François Le Lionnais, p. 481, Paris: Albert Blanchard, 1962.

*Ibid, p. 483.

binary composition, probably less strong but also, perhaps, more subtle than a composition based on one diagonal. But remember that no theory or regulating diagram can do your work for you: a creator must ultimately rely on his own judgment, or esthetic feeling, and not permit mechanical devices to take command.'"*

In his book *Vers une architecture* Le Corbusier defines the term as follows:

"A regulating diagram is a way of ensuring ourselves against what is arbitrary: it is a testing device to check a work that has been conceived with passion; it is the schoolboy's *'preuve par neuf,'** the mathematician's Q.E.D.

"A regulating diagram satisfies our spiritual needs by enabling us to seek ingenious and harmonious relationships. It makes a work eurythmic.

"A regulating diagram offers a tangible form of mathematics, the welcome sense of a visible order. The choice of a regulating diagram determines the basic geometry of a piece of work, one of its principal characteristics. The choice of a regulating diagram is one of the decisive moments of inspiration; it is an essential procedure in architecture." (3, p. 57)

The regulating diagrams, in and of themselves, are merely corrective instruments; the choice of the proper system is the creative act:

"There is no hard and fast, easily applicable formula for using regulating diagrams; it is really a question of inspiration, of true creativity. One has to discover the latent geometric law that governs and determines the character of a design. At a certain moment it will spring to mind and unify all the parts. There will be a few adjustments, a few corrections, and a perfect harmony will finally prevail." (7, p. 38)

In his book *Le Modulor* Le Corbusier gives the following examples:

"Figures A, B, C, D, and E show some of my pictorial or architectural works that, from 1918 on, were based on various regulating diagrams: 'the place of the right angle,' the Golden Section, the logarithmic spiral, the pentagon. . . . Each of these geometric systems provides a specific kind of equilibrium and, consequently, character. A regulating diagram is not, by nature, a preconceived format; the architect chooses one type or another in accordance with the character of his design. The regulating process, based on a geometric equilibrium, thus merely orders, clarifies, and purifies a design that has already been drawn up. A regulating diagram does not supply poetic or lyrical ideas, it does not inspire themes, and it does not create. It is a source of equilibrium. It is a tool for solving plastic problems. (26, p. 34)

Commenting further on his use of regulating diagrams for the Villa at Garches, he explains:

"The design of the entire house was governed by rigorous regulating diagrams that had the effect of modifying the dimensions of the various parts—sometimes by one centimeter (less than 1/2 in.). In a case like this mathematical laws

---

* *Le Corbusier et P. Jeanneret—2e Série,* p. 14, Paris: Albert Morancé, 1929.

**A simple method of checking multiplication problems.

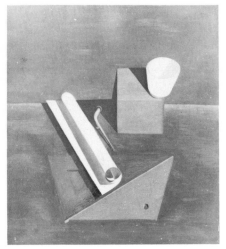

A   1919 Still life with a white bowl

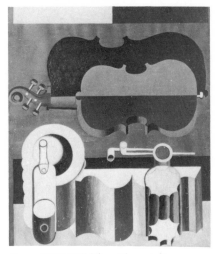

B   1920 Still life with a violin

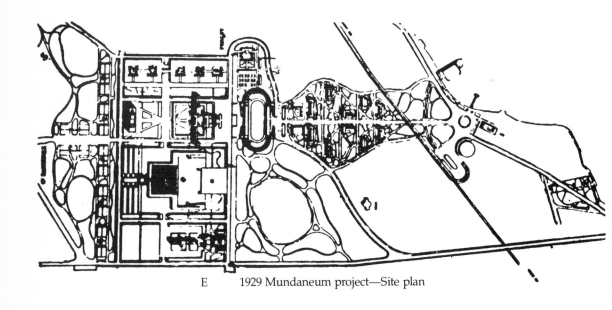

E   1929 Mundaneum project—Site plan

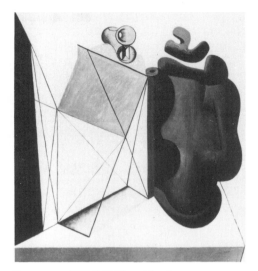

C   1930 Still life with a lantern

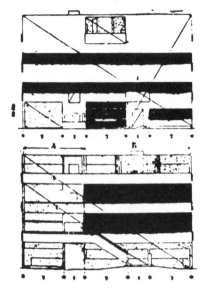

D   1927 Villa at Garches

are reassuring: when your work is finished, you know it is exactly right."* (Fig. 43)

"The north facade is governed by diagonals. But there are three horizontal strips of solid wall between the openings. Their respective widths seemed to form a numerical progression. Closer inspection showed that it was actually a 1, 2, 4 progression. A slight modification of the drawing made the progression more exact. This is an example of a *numerical diagram*.

"Furthermore, for structural reasons, the concrete posts were placed at regular intervals. Looking at the facade, one is constantly aware of the numerical measurements governing this structure. So, at Garches, in addition to the two preceding diagrams (the diagonals and the 1-2-4 progression), there is a third, so to speak, *built-in* diagram provided by the structural frame. It gives a 2-1-2-1-2 cadence.

"The south facade is also based on diagonals. This led to an interesting adjustment of the drawing. I am talking about the staircase leading down to the garden, which is parallel to the diagonal of the facade. To obtain this result, I had to raise the ground at the bottom of the stairs slightly. Subtleties of this kind count.

"Finally, another extremely important regulating diagram gives a quality of

*Le Corbusier et Pierre Jeanneret, Oeuvre complète de 1910–1929, by W. Boesiger and O. Stonorov, p. 144, Zurich: Erlenbach, 1937, and Artemis.

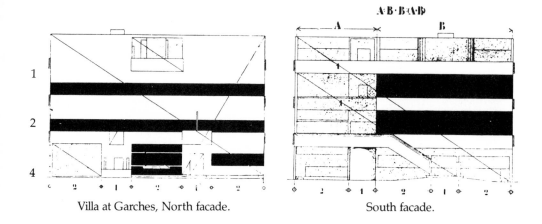

A·B·B:(A·B)

Villa at Garches, North facade.   South facade.

Fig. 43

rigorous precision to the dominant rhythm of this facade. I am talking about the relationship that ties the width of the west side of the facade (A) to that of the adjoining side (B)—the two most important elements of the composition. This relationship is based on the famous proportion, used in all great historical periods, called the *Golden Section*. If I wish to divide the length of the building into two segments, the Golden Section provides a dividing point that is mathematically exact, *the only dividing point* that can create such a subtle proportion. I could, for example, have divided the facade into two equal parts, or given it a 1-2 or 2-3 proportion, but these divisions sometimes look banal or slack. Not always, however. Here again, one has to use one's judgment."*

GOLDEN SECTION

Let us review briefly the properties of this "famous proportion" expressed by the formula noted on the drawing above (Fig. 43). A:B = B:(A+B). If we divide a straight line into two segments, A and B, so that $\frac{A}{B} = \frac{B}{(A+B)}$, or $\frac{B}{A} = \frac{(A+B)}{B}$, we find the ratio $\frac{B}{A}$ equals $\frac{1+\sqrt{5}}{2}$, or approximately 1.618. This number is represented by the Greek Letter ϕ.

If we extend the line beyond segment B with a segment equal to (A + B), we obtain a series of three lengths, A, B, and (A + B). This is the beginning of

Le Corbusier et P. Jeanneret—2e Série, pp. 15 et 16, Paris: Albert Morancé, 1929.

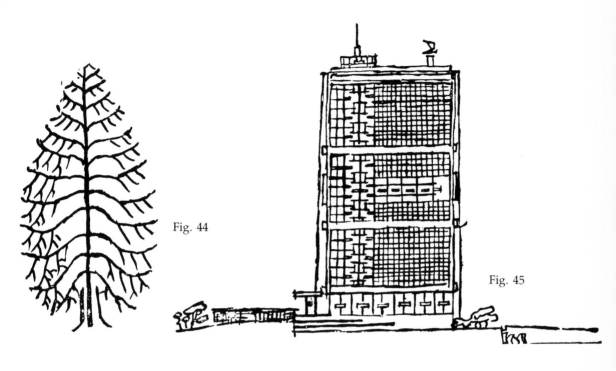

Fig. 44

Fig. 45

a "Golden Series," a geometric progression based on the ratio ϕ, where each term equals the sum of the two previous terms. It is the only series in which the terms are related both by multiplication and by addition.

In the series of whole numbers 0, 1, 1, 2, 3, 5, 8, 13, etc., where each number is the sum of the two preceding numbers, the ratio between two consecutive numbers tends toward ϕ. This series, discovered in the twelfth century by the Italian mathematician Fibonacci, is an approximate version of a Golden Series.

Le Corbusier again used the Golden Section in the design of his "Cité d'Affaires" in Algiers. As he suggests, it creates the same combination of unity and variety that exists in natural organisms:

"Natural organisms teach a valuable lesson: unified forms, pure silhouettes. The secondary elements are distributed on a graduated scale that ensures variety as well as unity. The system, which branches out to its furthest extremities, is a whole" (Fig. 44).

Speaking of the "Cité d'Affaires":

"Here the Golden Section prevails: it has supplied the harmonious envelope and sparkling prism; it has regulated the cadence on a human scale, permitted variations, authorized fantasies, governed the general character from top to bottom. This 150-meter-high (492 ft.) building is insured against

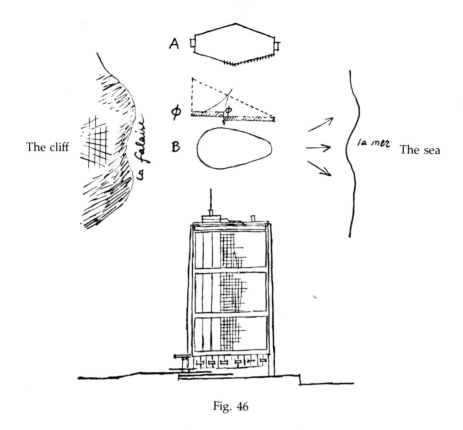

Fig. 46

all risks: it is harmonious in every part. And it is bound to harmonize with our sensibility" (Fig. 45). (18, p. 147)

Le Corbusier also shows how the Golden Section changed the character of the facade:

"Everything seemed to be governed, inexorably, by a succession of rational judgments. A poetic decision intervened. The plan was rigorously symmetrical. But after a rectification resulting from a Golden Section diagram, the character of the facade became asymmetric. The form seems to swell out on the left and taper off on the right, responding to the dual pressure of the site: the cliff and the sea (Fig. 46)." (18, p. 151)

In other words, the dividing line between small louvers and large louvers was shifted left of center so that the division of the facade corresponds with the proportion of the Golden Section (ϕ). Thus, although the plan remained symmetrical (A), the off-center division of the facade creates an illusion of asymmetry (B).

MODULOR

Le Corbusier's study of the Golden Section led to his development of the "Modulor", a system of related proportions, which he describes as follows:

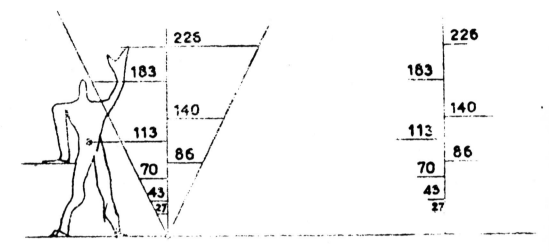

Fig. 47

"The Modulor is a measuring tool based on the human body and mathematics. *The height of a man with an upraised arm may be divided into segments at the points determining his position in space*—his feet, his solar plexus, his head, his fingertips. These three intervals produce a series of the Golden Section. . . ." (26, p. 55)

The principle of the Golden Section is here used to derive two series of dimensions from the human figure. One (the "Blue Series") is based on the height of a standing man with upraised arm: 2.26 meters (7 ft. 5 in.). The other (the "Red Series") is based on the height of this man measured from his feet to the top of his head: 1.83 meters (6 ft.) (Fig. 47).

Le Corbusier believed that these concrete measures, directly related to those of the human body, would help architects adapt their structures to human requirements.

"The numbers of the Modulor, which are chosen from an infinite number of possible values, are *measures*, which is to say real, bodily facts. To be sure, they belong to and have the advantages of the number system. But the constructions whose dimensions will be determined by these measures are *containers* or *extensions of man*.* We are more likely to choose the best measure-

*"A machine, a piece of furniture, and a newspaper are extensions of human gestures."

ments if we can see them, *appraise them with outstretched hands,* not merely imagine them (at least for measurements close to our own stature). The Modulor tape should thus lie on the architect's drafting board beside his compass so that, unrolled between his hands, it will offer him a direct view of the measures and, consequently, a concrete choice. Architecture (and, as previously mentioned, I apply the term to almost every man-made object) must appeal to our bodily senses as well as to our spirits and our minds." (26, p. 60)

The format of the Modulor is as follows:

"(1) *A tape* 2.26 meters (7 ft. 5 in.) long made of metal or plastic.* (2) *A table* giving useful numerical series. By *useful* I mean physically intelligible. This is limited to what we can apprehend as visible and tangible realities. We thought that measurements of more than 400 meters (1,300 ft.) can no longer be physically apprehended. . . . (3) *A booklet* containing an explanation of the Modulor and various resulting combinations." (26, p. 61)

Since the Modulor scale is given in both centimeters and inches, Le Corbusier hoped that it could serve as an international system of measurement. But he warns us not to expect too much of it:

". . . The Modulor is a working tool, a precision tool. You could think of it as a keyboard, a piano, a piano that has been *tuned.* The piano is in tune; how well you play on it depends on you and you alone. The Modulor does not give talent or, still less, genius. It does not sharpen dull wits. It gives its user the satisfaction of working with well-founded measurements. But out of the unlimited supply of Modulor combinations you are the one who has to make the choice." (26, p. 133)

Or again:

"The Modulor is a working tool *for those who create* (who compose—planners or designers) and not for those who build (masons, carpenters, mechanics, etc.)." (26, p. 180)

As in his discussion of regulating diagrams, Le Corbusier points out that the Modulor should not be used to determine the proportions of a building but to express the character of these proportions. This, as he constantly emphasizes, is a matter of personal judgment:

"Just as a painter who uses a regulating diagram must decide which part of his picture it is to govern, an architect who uses a regulating diagram, or in this case the Modulor scale, must decide which structural element of his building it is to govern. The problem, in either case, is to give careful consideration to the things you see. You see lines, surfaces, or volumes that call for the subtlety of proportioning. Where is the subject? What is the subject? The empty spaces in a room or the thickness of a wall? Which part of a window should be emphasized: the glazing or the surrounding frame? This is, each time, a question of personal judgment." (30, p. 105)

---

*One side of this tape gives the full-scale graduations of the Red and Blue series. The other side of the tape shows graduations in two different scales: one for architectural projects and one for urban planning projects.

In defending the Golden Section, on which the Modulor is based, Le Corbusier comments:

"Never mind if modern mathematicians consider the formulas of the Golden Section banal! Banality may well be the very thing we should be looking for, that is, a harmonious coexistence: *man-in-his-environment*, not interplanetary man or theory-making man. We build cities, houses, and equipment that are intended for men and will be manipulated and used by men.
"And man, as constituted by the dimensions of the bodily members that determine his position in space as he goes about his everyday activities, proceeds from the ratio ϕ." (30, p. 150)

Le Corbusier sums up his ideas on harmony with the example of the Ronchamp Chapel:

"I am, generally speaking, opposed to modules when they get in the way of the imagination and, in pursuing absolutes, end up by paralyzing invention. But I believe that (poetic) relationships are absolute. And relationships are by definition variable, diverse, innumerable. . . . I refuse to accept canons; harmonious relationships are what I am looking for.
"When the Ronchamp Chapel is finished, in the spring of 1955, it will perhaps show that architecture is not concerned with columns; it is concerned with plastic events. And plastic events are not subject to scholastic or academic formulas; they are self-determined and unlimited in number." (30, p. 264)

Speaking of the Ronchamp Chapel, he says, "Hand-written over the facade is: Modulor throughout," but, nonetheless, warns us of possible dangers:

"I really enjoyed playing with the possibilities of the Modulor, at the same time watching the game out of the corner of my eye to avoid blunders. For blunders are always lying in wait for us, holding out their hands to us, catching hold of our coattails, dragging us into the abyss." (30, p. 267)

CHAPTER V
How to Teach Architecture

LE CORBUSIER'S IDEAS on this subject are, for the most part, presented in two books: *Sur les quatre routes (The Four Routes)* (1941), a study of urban planning, and *Précisions (Further Remarks)* (1930), written after his trip to South America.

Sur les quatre routes proposes a general reform of architectural education; *Précisions* describes how Le Corbusier would go about teaching architecture.

THE REFORM

He himself had no formal architectural training:

> "I never studied architecture in a school. Here, as in all things, even sports, I taught myself. Until I was thirty-five, this was often an agonizing experience; I would not wish it on most people." (20, last chapter).

Indeed, he was strongly opposed to the teaching methods of existing architectural schools, in particular the French Ecole des Beaux-Arts. His "reform" proposes an alternate method of instruction: teach technical subjects in schools but let students learn design by working in an architectural firm of their choice. He instituted this system in his own office in Paris:

> "I think I have the right to say that I know what young people are like. I have always refused to teach, for my experience, in 1911–12, in an avant-garde school showed me that I was not intended to be a teacher. Nonetheless,

during the last fifteen years almost 200 young people have passed through our office on the rue de Sèvres, bringing to our studies and our work the invaluable contribution of their enthusiasm and eagerness to learn. I was never tempted to make pedagogical speeches to them. I never interfered with their ideas, great or small: youth is obscure, complex, uncertain, timid, unconscious, intuitive. . . . Young people (though this rarely happens) may have highly original temperaments, but if they enter the field of architecture and urban planning, one that calls for an ability to appraise and combine human things, to decide about human needs, they will have to wait.

"One can be a poet at twenty, a virtuoso at fifteen; but architects and urban planners are late bloomers."

According to Le Corbusier, this is one of the great disadvantages of teaching architectural design in schools:

"What do schools do? They give assignments. . . . The teacher criticizes the student's work. How can he cut into the living flesh of this muddled confession—a young person's project—without inflicting cruel bruises and serious wounds? There remains the possibility of speaking immortal words. This brings us to the verge of the abyss: slogans and catchwords unworthy of a serious enterprise like architecture, which must combine so many different factors: stability, economy; how to organize the plan and section spatially; how to make the succession of interior and exterior volumes, in their unity and their efficiency, sing."

Still worse, schools blind their students to these architectural realities by teaching them to make attractive drawings:

". . . One day, at Rio de Janeiro, Mr. Capanema, minister of national education and public health, asked me how I would conceive an architectural school.

"The reform, I answered, is to free architecture from drawings. Drawings are made indoors, with docile instruments. . . . They may, on the one hand, be simple stenographic notations of architectural ideas that determine spaces and specify the proper materials. This art is produced by a controlling mind, by an imagination that unfolds the forms before the architect's very eyes, the skillful, correct, magnificent play. . . . They may, on the other hand, be a shimmering display of illustrations, illuminations, colors, clever stagings, that will have the effect of blinding the author no less than the observer to the realities that he is dealing with.

"Good architecture is expressed on paper by a working drawing so bare that its character is visible only to the inner eye. This piece of paper is an act of faith in the architect, who knows what he is doing. It has no commercial value, nor will it help obtain a diploma. . . . The flattering illustrations of ambitious architects, conversely, titillate their eager clients. *Drawings are, in effect, the booby trap of architecture.*

"The aim of this reform is to make architecture true to the purposes it serves, the dimensions it describes, the materials it uses. The problem at hand must be concisely stated and concisely solved. Stone, reinforced concrete, steel, and wood react quite differently to compression and tension, and a drawing should express these very different reactions. An elegant solution strives for economy of means. The game we are to play is bounded, on one side, by this economy and, on the other, by the splendor of the result." (17, pp. 163–166)

Le Corbusier had already stressed this point in his reply (1935) to the questionnaire of an American architect, Percival Goodman:

"I have never been able to tolerate schools. This is basically because of my difficult character but also, and more especially, because I built my first house, from A to Z, when I was eighteen. (It was very carefully detailed and very complicated.) I have always had the weight of stones and bricks in my arms, the astonishing resistance of wood in my eyes, the miraculous properties of steel in my mind. . . . And I felt that there were different kinds of drawings on the drafting board.

"Which is to say that similar spaces or thicknesses have different potentialities, depending on whether they are to be made of stone, brick, wood, or steel; that each material has a characteristic emotional, no less than physical, force; and, all in all, that architectural design should always stay close to matter or materials.

"I have always been, and today still am, struck with childlike amazement at the unexpected possibilities of matter. I feel that these possibilities, and we have only a rough idea of a small part of them, will point the way to a new mode of construction. Once architects have been brought into daily contact with industry (workshops and engineers), they will gain new strength. And architecture will take its place in the construction process, bringing that harmonious and well-proportioned arrangement of materials that results in the creation of living works." (13, p. 301)

"Technical subjects—the exact sciences—will of course continue to be taught in qualified schools, but exact sciences are only a part of architecture. That the Buenos Aires School of Exact Sciences includes architecture means one of two things: the school is either misnamed, or it has the wrong curriculum. For ideas, motivations, and intentions are not exact sciences."

The teachers, chosen by the students, will be directly involved in contemporary building and urban planning problems:

". . . They will be 'many and manifold' because architecture and urban planning will have branched out in many directions. Since they will be practicing architects, not schoolteachers, they will accept only suitable applicants. Those who are ultimately rejected will learn that they were not intended to be architects before it is too late. The teachers chosen in this way will no longer have permanent tenure. . . . Their reputation will be determined by their value. If a teacher's reputation declines, his office will be depopulated. If, on the contrary, his office gets too crowded, he will be able to select the best candidates.

"The system here proposed is none other than the traditional workshop of former times. It connects us with that era prior to the institution of architectural schools, which produced real architecture.

"Diplomas will be based on examinations in exact sciences. There can be no diploma for ideas, motivations, or intentions. So there will be engineering diplomas instead of architectural diplomas? Why not? Several countries al-

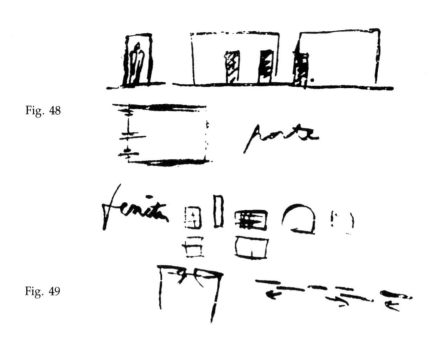

Fig. 48

Fig. 49

ready give architects the title of engineer. A sliding scale of techniques can easily be established. It may be objected that we might just as well keep the existing schools that to a great extent serve the same purpose. But schools have killed architecture. My proposed reform would, on the contrary, revive it. . . . For the renewal of the teaching body would be determined from the ground up under the pressure of that which is always new, still uncompromised by, unentangled in, the struggle for existence: youth." (17, pp. 166–168)

HOW WOULD I GO ABOUT TEACHING ARCHITECTURE?

Le Corbusier replied, at considerable length, to this question, asked of him during one of his 1929 Buenos Aires lectures to a group of architects, architectural students, and engineers. As usual, he contrasts sterile academic formulas with the actual experience of architecture:

"*How would I go about teaching architecture?*
"I would begin by forbidding 'orders,'* by putting an end to this disease, this scandal, this unbelievable insult to human intelligence. I would demand that *architecture be respected.*
"On the other hand, I would tell my students that the Acropolis in Athens

---

*These "orders," Doric, Ionic, Corinthian, etc., were still studied in certain architectural schools of the time.

74

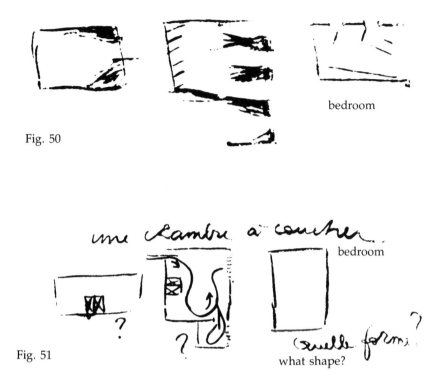

bedroom

Fig. 50

une chambre à coucher

bedroom

Fig. 51
what shape?

is a stirring spectacle, and that they will one day understand its unique greatness. I would promise to explain the magnificence of the Farnese Palace and the spiritual hiatus between the apses of St. Peter's and its facade, both of which were built on the same order but in one case by Michelangelo and in the other by Alberti, and to explain many other great instances of architectural purity and probity. However, such things cannot be understood without a certain amount of experience. Nobility, purity, and the immortality of proportion: these, I would tell them, constitute the great and deep delights of architecture, as all can see."

In the meantime:

"I would always make my teaching as concrete as possible. I would strive to give my students a strong sense of personal control, of self-determination, the 'how' and the 'why' I have been speaking of. I would implore them to cultivate this attitude tirelessly throughout their lives. I would like them to apply this sense of being in control to concrete facts. Facts are fluid and mutable, especially in the present time. I would teach them to despise formulas. I would tell them *proportions are all that matter.*

"Let's go back to our sketches:

"I would ask young students: How do you make a door? What are its dimensions? Where will you put it (Fig. 48)?

"How do you make a window? And, incidentally, what is a window for? Do you really know why we make windows? If so, you'll be able to tell me

75

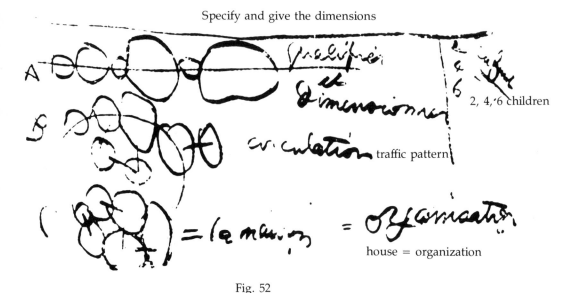

Specify and give the dimensions

2, 4, 6 children

traffic pattern

house = organization

Fig. 52

why we make arched, square, and rectangular windows (Fig. 49). I want the reasons. And I would add: watch out! Do we still need windows?

"In what part of a room do you make a doorway? Why here rather than there? Ha! You seem to have several solutions? You're right; there *are* several solutions, and each gives a different architectural sensation. Ha! You realize that these different solutions lie at the very basis of architecture! The different ways you enter a room, as determined by the position of the door, produce different sensations and change the character of the wall. You can feel that this is what architecture is. But I forbid you to draw an axis on your plan: those formulas are eyewash.

"Another equally important problem: where are you going to put your window? Do you realize that the different places where light bursts into a room produce different sensations (Fig. 50)? Well, draw all the possible places for window openings and tell me which are best.

"As a matter of fact, why did you draw a room of this shape? Find other *workable* shapes and put doors and windows in them all. You'd better buy a big notebook for this kind of work; you'll need a lot of pages" (Fig. 51).

"Now draw up all the possible shapes of a dining room, a kitchen, a bedroom, each with its adjoining services. Then try to reduce them to the smallest size compatible with perfect functioning. A kitchen? You will see that this is a problem of urban design—traffic flow and work spaces. Don't forget that the kitchen is the vital center of the house.

"Now draw a businessman's office; his secretary's, his typists', the engineers'. Remember that as a house is a *machine for living,* an office building is a machine for working.

"You don't know what 'orders' are. Nor the 1920s style. If I catch you drawing any 1920s style, I'll box your ears. You must not draw anything that is a drawing. You are fitting parts together; you are supplying equipment; that's all."

Le Corbusier suggests that students study the exact functioning of a house in organizational diagrams:

"Now try to solve one of the trickiest of all contemporary problems: the smallest possible house.

"First for a single man or woman. Then for a young married couple. . . . Then your family moves to another house; they have two children.

"Study a house for a family with four children.

"Since this is all very difficult, begin by drawing a straight line and string the necessary spaces on it, one after the other, in the order of their successive functions. And make each space as small as possible (Fig. 52).

"Then make a flow diagram so you'll know which rooms to put next to one another.

"And, finally, try to fit these spaces together to make a house. (Forget about the structure, which is a different problem.) If you happen to like chess, this will be right up your alley!"

When the student starts studying technical problems, Le Corbusier advises him to visit construction sites:

"Go to construction sites to see how reinforced concrete, roof slabs, and floors are made, how windows are set in. I'll give you a pass. Make sketches. If you see any stupid mistakes, be sure to note them down. When you get back, ask me some questions. Don't believe that mathematics teaches you how to construct a building. That's an old academic nostrum.

"You'll have to study a certain amount of statics.* It's easy. Don't feel obliged to understand exactly how the formulas of the mechanics of materials were figured out by mathematicians. If you make the effort, you will understand the mechanism of these computations, but it's more important to remember how the different parts of a building work. Try to understand what the moment of inertia** really means. Once you have grasped the principle, you'll feel free to do anything you want. These problems have nothing to do with mathematics. Leave mathematics to the mathematicians. But you're not through yet.

"You'll have to study acoustics, thermal insulation, expansion, heating, and air-conditioning. The more you learn about these things, the better off you will be later on."

Students must also study circulation problems:

"Now draw this long wharf, then the buoys that mark the channel (Fig. 53). Show how a 200-meter-long (656 ft.) steamer docks, how it undocks. You'll only need to cut the rough shape of a ship out of colored paper and

---

*The branch of mechanics dealing with forces in equilibrium.
**A measure of the stiffness of structural members.

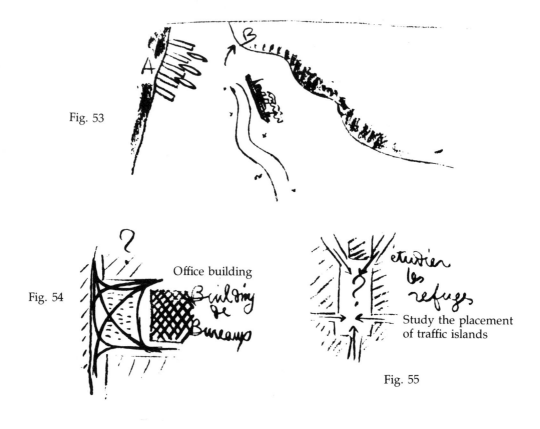

Fig. 53

Fig. 54

Office building

Fig. 55

Study the placement
of traffic islands

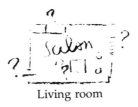

Living room

Fig. 56

show its various positions on your drawing. You may get some ideas about planning docking facilities.

"Let's draw an office building; in front there's a parking area for cars; there are 200 offices in the building (Fig. 54). Try to find out how many parking spaces will be needed. As with the steamer, show the maneuvering patterns clearly. You may get some ideas about the best shape for the islands, the best dimensions and shape for parking spaces, their access to and from the street.

"The following piece of advice is worth its weight in gold: use colored pencils. Color will help you distinguish, classify, clearly see, and read the lines. It will let you handle the situation. If you use only black pencil, you'll get bogged down and lose control. Always say to yourself: *this must be clearly legible*. Color will save you.

"Here is a city square where several streets meet (Fig. 55). Try to understand how the cars pass each other. Try to imagine all sorts of squares. Decide which ones permit the best traffic flow.

"Take the plan of a living room—the doors and the windows. Arrange the necessary pieces of furniture so they can be used to best advantage; this involves traffic patterns, common sense, and many other things! Ask yourself: Does it work" (Fig. 56)?

The student must also make surveys of existing facilities, measure their dimensions, and try to understand their functioning.

"Now I'm going to ask for some written work. Make a comparative, analytic study showing why cities like Buenos Aires, La Plata, Mar del Plata, and Avejanella are as they are. It's quite a difficult task for a student. But it will teach you that before you start drawing anything you must always know what it's about, how it works, and what it's for. It's a good way to develop your judgment.

"Go down to the station sometime, measuring tape in hand, and make an accurate survey of a dining car, both the dining area and the kitchen, with their traffic problems. Do the same thing for a sleeping car.

"Then go down to the harbor and visit an ocean liner. Make colored plans and sections, showing how it works. Incidentally, do you know exactly what happens on a liner? Do you know that it's a palace for 2,000 people, a third of whom require a luxurious way of life? Do you know that it contains a hotel system for three entirely independent, separate classes; a gigantic system of mechanical propulsion, with its staff and team of engineers; and, finally, a navigational system, with its officers and sailors? When you can express clearly the organization of a liner in colored plans and sections, you'll be able to enter the next competition for the League of Nations. You'll be able to draw up the plans of a palace."

Finally, the student must learn to see:

"And now, my good friends and students, I implore you to *keep your eyes open*.

"Do you keep your eyes open? Are you trained to keep your eyes open? Do you know how to keep your eyes open? Do you always keep them open? What do you look at when you walk around the city? In Buenos Aires you all say: We have nothing; our city is completely new. Architects send for European journals and books on architecture. They then proudly show us

open your eyes

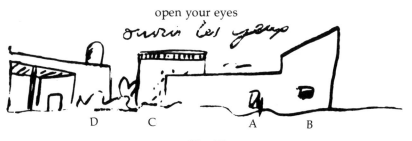

Fig. 57

spirit of truth/lie

Fig. 58

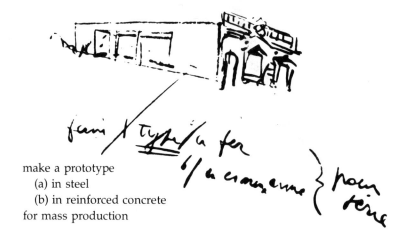

make a prototype
  (a) in steel
  (b) in reinforced concrete
for mass production

Fig. 59

little clusters of English cottages set in a sea of little Buenos Aires houses. Why do those cottages feel like a slap in the face?

"Look, I'm drawing a wall with a door in it (A); the wall is extended by the gable of a lean-to with a little window (B) in the middle; on the left I draw a loggia, very square, very simple (C). I put this delightful cylinder on the roof (D) of a house: it's a water tank (Fig. 57). You think: well, now he's designing a modern village! Not at all; I'm drawing the houses of Buenos Aires. There are at least 50,000 of them. They are built every day—by Italian contractors. They are a very logical expression of the life of Buenos Aires. Their dimensions are correct; their form is harmonious; they are skillfully related to each other. This is your vernacular; it was there fifty years ago, and it's still there today. You tell me: We have nothing! I reply: You do have something: a standard plan and a play of beautiful forms in the Argentinian light. Look! Don't you see that these English cottages are scandalous! Their unusable high-pitched tile roofs merely lead to garret rooms and higher maintenance costs. You naturally used flat roofs in Argentina, but books on European architecture are senselessly dragging you back three centuries: look at your 'model' garden-cities and resort towns at Mar del Plata!"

"The other day, at sundown, I took a long walk in the streets of La Plata with Gonzales Garraño. There were garden walls, like, for example, this (E) (Fig. 58). That little door stuck in the wall is an *architectural fact* (F). *The other architectural fact* is this door cutting the wall in two (G). *The third architectural fact* is this big garage door (H). *The fourth architectural fact* is this narrow passage between the two properties with the garden wall on one side and the mass of the lean-to on the other (I). *The fifth architectural fact* is the sloping roof and the overhang of the lean-to (J)."

Le Corbusier warns students against architectural lies:

"Ha! You're shaking with laughter because I'm drawing a windmill made of iron, the mill that's always turning beside Argentinian houses. You think that I'm going to denigrate this mill because it's not Doric, Ionic, Corinthian, or Tuscan but simply ironwork. Let me tell you, when you design a house, first draw an ironwork windmill. Your house will look well if it ties in with the windmill, which is an honest being!

"I implore you to steep yourself in *the spirit of truth*.

"Watch out! Now I'm going to undermine my eulogy of Italian contractors. The sketches I just made were rear views of houses. This was all that was needed. Well, out front, on the street, where you put the house number and name, where you tell visitors 'This is my house,' the contractor had recourse to Mr. Vignola and his 'orders.'* What a monstrosity! A fine little South American pastry shop (Fig. 59)! And since the house was, after all, fairly unpretentious, since it was not tall enough, the Italian contractor added a balustrade, often bearing a large escutcheon. On that, I inscribe the word *lie*.

"Keep your eyes open when you go behind the houses and close them when you are in the street!

"This said, I would give my student the following problem: go and make

---

*Iacopo Barozzi, called Il Vignola, a sixteenth-century Italian architect, published a *Treatise on the Five Orders of Architecture*.

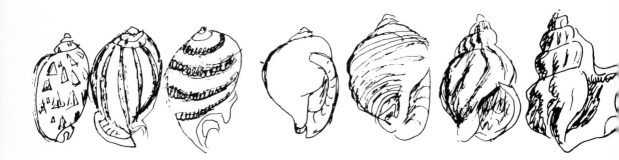

Fig. 60

surveys of the honest houses behind the facades. You will study this type of vernacular to see whether it can be adapted to mass production, in steel (dry wall construction), for example, or in reinforced concrete (precast panels)."

Le Corbusier again warns against the pitfall of skillful drawings:

"Now that I have appealed to your *sense of truth*, I would like you, since you are studying architecture, to develop *a loathing for drawings*. For drawing is nothing more than covering a piece of paper with engaging things like styles, 'orders,' *fashions*. Whereas architecture, which exists in space, in breadth, in depth, and in height, consists of volumes and traffic patterns. It is created *in the mind*. You must therefore learn to conceive it in your mind, with closed eyes; you will then know how it is going to turn out. The piece of paper only serves to express your idea so that you can transmit it to your client and your contractor. Everything depends on the plan and the section. When you have created a simple, working organism with the plan and section, *you will have your facade*; and if you have a certain feeling for harmonious relationships, your facade may well stir our emotions. Bear in mind that houses are made to be lived in. Well and good. But you will not be a good architect unless your facades are beautiful, and this is purely a matter of proportions. You will need a great deal of imagination to succeed here; the simpler the problem, the greater the need."(9, pp. 221-231)

Le Corbusier believed that architects could develop their imagination by studying natural organisms:

"Go to the Museum of Natural History and study a class of shells (Fig. 60). You will learn the infallible law of unity, variety, and harmony. In the middle of the series is a standard shell of uniform color and neutral texture, which expresses a perfect equilibrium. The more highly modeled variations on the right range from the most restrained to the most violent kind of sculpture. The greater the relief, the more monochrome and uniform the texture. The smooth-textured series on the left becomes increasingly shiny and brilliant: first pure white enamel, then sharply outlined stripes following the horizontal and vertical contours, then combining both in checkered, dotted, diagonal or diamond-shaped decorations, etc. . . .

"Friends, nature sometimes whispers: look here!

"Contemporary architecture and urban design are opening up in every direction with an unlimited wealth of possibilities; so when you get back from the Museum of Natural History, look on your builder's palette for the materials whose specific characteristics best answer your subtlest intentions."*

Since early boyhood, Le Corbusier had drawn shells, rocks, trees, plants, pine cones, and lizards—and advises others to do the same:

". . . How can we increase our creative power? Not by subscribing to architectural journals, but by adventuring into the inexhaustible realm of natural riches. This is where we can really learn architecture and, to begin with, grace! Yes, flexibility, precision, the unquestionable reality of all those harmonious creations, apparent everywhere in nature. From inside to outside serene perfection prevails; in plants, animals, sites, seas, plains, or mountains; even in the perfect harmony of natural catastrophes, geological cataclysms, etc. Keep your eyes open! If you wholeheartedly commit yourself to this study of the reason of things, you will inevitably arrive at architecture.

". . . I would like architects—not just students—to pick up a pencil and draw a plant, a leaf, the spirit of a tree, the harmony of a sea shell, formations of clouds, the complex play of waves spreading out on a beach, so as to discover different expressions of an inner force. I would like their hands and minds to become passionately involved in this kind of intimate investigation."*

---

*L'Architecture d'aujourd'hui, numéro spécial, 1948, p. 53.

*Letter from Le Corbusier to Mr. Martienssen in Johannesburg, dated September 23, 1936.

CHAPTER VI
Housing

Architecture or Revolution

In 1923 Le Corbusier considered housing an urgent social as well as architectural problem. The last chapter of his book *Vers une architecture*, entitled "Architecture or Revolution," stresses this point:

"In all branches of industry new problems have been raised, and tools for solving them have been created. History shows that this is a revolution.

"In the building industry we have begun to make factory-produced parts; we are successfully mass-producing small and large units to meet new economic needs. History shows that the methods and scope of building enterprises have been revolutionized.

"Architecture has evolved slowly over the centuries, following the development of structure and ornamentation, but in the last fifty years steel and cement have produced new techniques. These have created powerful construction methods and, at the same time, undermined the existing premises of architecture. History shows that 'styles' have no further meaning and that a contemporary style has evolved. A revolution has occurred.

"As people have consciously or unconsciously become aware of these events and new needs have consciously or unconsciously arisen, the social mechanism has been *profoundly shaken*. It oscillates between a radical reform and a catastrophe.

"A need for shelter is the primary instinct of every living being, but the most active segments of society, workers or intellectuals, *are no longer decently housed.* Building is the answer to the present disturbance of the social equilibrium: we must choose between architecture and revolution." (3, p. 227)

And again:

"Disturbed by the pressures assailing him on every side, contemporary man is conscious, on the one hand, of a world developing around him in a regular, logical, intelligible way, which produces useful and usable things, and, on the other hand, of the frustration of living in an antiquated, hostile setting. This setting is his shelter: his town, his street, his house, and his apartment have turned against him and, because they are unusable, prevented him from pursuing in his leisure hours the human goals pursued during his working hours, prevented him from obeying the organic principle of his being—which is to found a family and, as all animals and all men at all times have done, develop an organized family life. As a result, society is watching the destruction of the family and, horror stricken, realizes that this will bring about its own destruction." (3, p. 241)

As here suggested, Le Corbusier viewed housing and urban planning as a single problem—the problem of human shelter—and it is often difficult to distinguish between them in his writings. In the interest of clarity, I have nonetheless treated them in separate chapters.

Reflections on "The Machine for Living"

In a 1921 *L'Esprit nouveau* article, Le Corbusier wrote:

"A house is a machine for living. We must have sunlight, bathrooms, hot and cold water, controlled temperature, proper food storage, healthy conditions, and the beauty of good proportions." (3, p. 73)

Le Corbusier's definition of a house as a "machine for living" is widely known, but it is not generally remembered that the definition refers to esthetic pleasure as well as to functional efficiency, i.e., to "the beauty of good proportions":

"The reading of a work, which is really what the word *architecture* means, goes beyond immediate physical sensations. It reveals the dazzling clarity and inexhaustible fertility of the intention behind the work. And as the creative act is reconstituted step by step in the observer's mind, his admiration is substantiated.

"How far we seem to have soared above toilets and central heating, above the 'machine for living'!

"But this is not really so. If we still believe that man has a heart and a head, we have remained in the very center of the machine for living." (8, p. 5).

He later explained why he had used this term:

"In 1920 I recognized the fundamental importance of a house by calling it a 'machine for living' and thus demanding it answer to a well-formulated question fully and exactly. It is an entirely human concept, making man the central concern of architecture."*

---

*L'Homme et l'architecture, 11–12, 13, 14, 1947, p. 7.

Plate 15: Carthusian monastery of Ema.

Plate 16: "Domino" housing project.

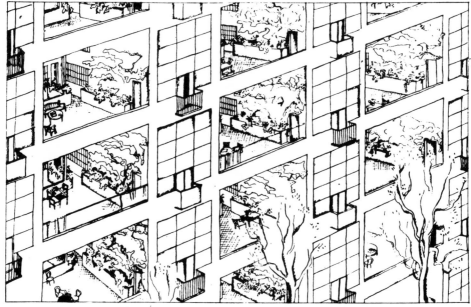

Plate 17: "Immeuble-villas," detail of facade.

"We must, in effect, house people . . . which means provide for:
(a) well-lit floors,
(b) protection against intruders, weather, etc.,
(c) the most convenient traffic flow among the various furnishings of the apartment,
(d) a choice of furnishings adapted to present times.

"These different elements form a material organism that, in 1921 (*L'Esprit nouveau*), I named: a machine for living. The expression immediately caught on and is now hurled back at me. . . ." (9, p. 86)

Le Corbusier had written:

"We can no longer accept traditional houses, which misuse space. We must (this is a necessary consequence of present building costs) conceive a house as a machine for living, as a tool. . . . A house was hitherto conceived as an incoherent agglomeration of large rooms that were always oversized and, at the same time, cramped." (3, p. 200)

The furniture was as inefficient as the rooms.

"We cannot revise the plans of contemporary houses effectively unless we take a new look at the furniture question. This is the Gordian knot. . . .
"Furniture, apart from chairs and tables, consists almost entirely of storage space. And existing storage units generally have the wrong dimensions and are practically unusable. I condemn such a waste of space." (9, p. 105)

Plate 18: Housing project in Bordeaux, detail.

Plate 19: Housing project in Bordeaux, perspective view.

Apartment Buildings

Le Corbusier devoted many years to the problem of apartment buildings. He explains:

". . . It is based on a *human-scaled* unit. Let me show you the path which, after twenty years of eager curiosity, led me to the right solution.

"The initial germ of these studies was my 1907 visit to the Carthusian monastery of Ema, near Florence. I saw, in the harmonious countryside of Tuscany, a *modern city* crowning the top of a hill. The uninterrupted ring of monks' cells formed the noblest silhouette in the landscape. Each cell overlooks the plain and opens, at a lower level, into a small, enclosed garden. I thought I had never seen such happy living arrangements. At the back of each cell a door and a pass-through window open onto an arcaded street, which gives access to communal facilities for prayers, visits, meals, and burials." (9, p. 91)

It is important to realize that these "cells," like those of most Carthusian monasteries, are not single rooms. They are actually small, adjacent houses grouped around a central cloister. Each house has a bedroom, a workroom, an oratory, etc., and a little garden.

". . . This modern city dates from the fifteenth century. The radiant vision left an indelible impression. On my way home from Athens in 1910, I again stopped by the monastery." (9, p. 92)

The Carthusian monastery had indeed made a strong impression on Le Corbusier. His memory of the "radiant vision" resurfaced in his 1915 "Domino" project, 1922 "Immeuble-Villas," 1925 garden-city project in Bordeaux, and the "Unité d'Habitation" in Marseille, completed in 1952.

Le Corbusier explains:

"One day, in 1922, I told my partner, Pierre Jeanneret, about it [the monastery of Ema], and we immediately drew up a group of immeuble-villas on the back of a restaurant menu. The idea was born. Detailed plans appeared a few months later in our display of urban design at the Salon d'Automne under the heading 'A contemporary city for three million people.' " (9, p. 92)

What are these "immeuble-villas"?

"A hundred and twenty villas, each with its own garden, grouped together in a five-story building. Communal services are organized on a hotel basis, thus solving the servant problem (which is only beginning and reflects an irreversible social trend)." (3, p. 206)

The communal services, already promoted by Le Corbusier in 1922 and since incorporated into many apartment buildings, are as follows:

"The servants no longer necessarily live with the family. They come here, as they would come to a factory, to do a day's work, and an attentive staff is on twenty-four-hour duty. A purchasing service supplies raw or prepared foods, which leads to better quality at lower costs. A large kitchen provides meals for the apartments or for a communal restaurant.

"Each apartment has a small gym, but there is a large gymnasium and a 300-meter (328 yd.) track on the roof. There is also a lounge on the roof, which can be used by the residents.

"The usual cramped building entrance with the inevitable concierge's room is replaced by a large hall. Doormen on day and night duty admit visitors and show them to the elevators. There are tennis courts in the large courtyard on the roof of the underground garage." (3, p. 208)

Le Corbusier, remembering the cloister arcade, or "street," of the Ema monastery, calls the long hallways of his large apartment buildings "rues en l'air," or elevated streets:

"Let's go back to the Carthusian monastery of Ema and our immeuble-villas, two arrangements of cells built on a human scale. . . .

"I visualize a split-level cell with a double ceiling height. I make a *street* in the rear of the lower level, which will become an elevated street. . . . This *elevated street* is repeated vertically at 6-meter (20 ft.) intervals . . . I call it a *street* rather than a corridor . . . to stress that it is a means of horizontal circulation completely independent of the apartments that open onto it. These elevated streets lead at convenient intervals to groups of elevators, ramps, or stairs, which go down to ground level or up to the roof, with its solarium,

Fig. 61

swimming pool, gymnasium, and paths through the terrace gardens. In hilly areas there could also be a highway on the roof."* (9, p. 97)

Le Corbusier also devoted considerable thought to the problem of optimum ceiling heights in apartments:

"We must consider what ceiling height in the box that shelters us is, first, most *pleasing* and, second, most *efficient*. In the first place, the height must be adapted to our human gestures. . . . Secondly, the height must provide the right amount of air and sunlight. This can be determined by existing technology." (11, p. 51)

The idea of split-level apartments was first suggested to Le Corbusier by the plan of a small Paris restaurant:

". . . There was a bar and, in the rear, a kitchen; the space was divided vertically by a loft; the glazed front opened onto the street. One day we saw that the whole architectural setup could be used as a model for a house: a simplified window system (large glazed surfaces at each end), two lateral bearing walls, a flat roof on top."*

Le Corbusier used the idea in his 1919 "Citrohan" house (Fig. 61), a model for mass-produced houses, and later adapted it to apartment buildings.

At the 1925 *Exposition Internationale des Arts Décoratifs* in Paris, he built a full-size model of a split-level apartment, which he describes as follows:

---

*Le Corbusier is here referring to his 1929 proposals for the development of São Paulo and Rio de Janeiro.

*Le Corbusier et Pierre Jeanneret, *Oeuvre compléte de 1910–1929*, p. 31, by W. Boesiger and O. Stonorov, Zurich: Erlenbach, 1937, and Artemis.

"It is a double-height glazed room divided in the rear into two levels. I then remembered that my 1919 Citrohan house, designed for mass-production, already had the same plan. . . .

"The idea had materialized. It was supported by many examples of traditional or vernacular architecture and by our own successive experiments. From now on, urban-design projects are on a sure footing. The cell is alive, workable, beautiful, economic, efficient. With this brilliant cellular organization the city can grow taller. . . ." (11, p. 52)

Le Corbusier points out two advantages of split-level "cells" in tall apartment buildings. First, the available interior space is better used:

"If we accept the reduced height of 2.20 meters (7 ft. 3 in.) for certain living functions, we can give the rich *as well as the poor* the splendor, magnificence, and dignity of a living room 4.50 meters (14 ft. 9 in.) high: modern man will no longer have to live like a caged animal." (11, p. 54)

Second, these high living rooms allow large glazed surfaces on the facade that are well suited to the scale of tall buildings:

"I was standing on a Paris sidewalk, thinking that we would have to make tall buildings 50 meters high (160 ft.) in order to leave enough area on the ground for traffic and for our emotional needs (space, sky, and trees). I felt that windows spaced at 2.50-meter (8 ft.) intervals would create too small a grid for these tall buildings." (11, p. 52)

Le Corbusier, referring to his Marseille "Unité d'Habitation" (1947–1952), which was the final outcome of his twenty-five-year study of contemporary housing, remarked:

"Man's house, which was once a perfect container, can again aspire to harmony—and even to Palladio's smile. The only difference will be one of scale. Vertical garden-cities will help urban planners find rational and harmonious solutions."*

*Décor d'aujourd'hui, Paris, 1946, 35, p. 126.

CHAPTER VII
Urban Planning

LE CORBUSIER approached the field of urban planning more slowly than he did the field of architecture. His first article on the subject appeared in June 1922, in the seventeenth issue of *L'Esprit nouveau,* at a time when his general theory of architecture was already completely thought out. His ideas, fairly schematic to begin with, were developed gradually, with occasional alterations and revisions, over the following decades.

By 1922, Le Corbusier, aged thirty-five, had learned a good deal about architecture from a number of different sources: his training at a technical school, L'Ecole d'Art, at La Chaux-de-Fonds in Switzerland; the various architects, French, German, and Austrian, for whom he had worked; and his travels in Germany, Austria, and many Mediterranean countries.

He knew little about urban planning. Indeed, Le Corbusier would have had difficulty finding guidance in this nascent field. He had to start from scratch and was prompted to do so by his perception of the enormous problems of existing cities.

These problems had a long history: they had developed unchecked with the evolution of the city. In explaining this point, Le Corbusier distinguished between what he called "the donkey's way" and "the way of man":

"Man walks in a straight line because he has a goal; he knows where he's going. He decides to go somewhere and walks right up to it. A donkey ambles absentmindedly along, zigzagging to avoid large stones, skirt steep inclines, and stay in the shade. He exerts himself as little as possible.

"Man's feelings are governed by his reason; he subordinates his feelings and instincts to his goal. His intelligence gives orders to his animal nature. It establishes rules that are derived from practical experience, and experience is hard won. Man has to work in order to survive. And he cannot work effectively unless he follows a certain line of conduct, unless he obeys the rules derived from practical experience. He has to think ahead, toward the result.

"The donkey doesn't think about anything at all, except avoiding effort.

"The donkey marked out all our European cities, including Paris, unfortunately." (6, p. 5)

Le Corbusier, in a 1922 manifesto, formulated the underlying problems of existing cities:

"The survival of obsolete frameworks paralyzes city development. Industry and commerce will be strangled by backward cities.

"Traditionalism, in large cities, obstructs the development of transport, cramps and debilitates activity, kills progress, and discourages new ideas.

"The decay of old cities and present-day working pressures are causing physical and mental illness. Contemporary society must recover its spent forces. The layout of a city determines the physical and mental condition of its residents. Unhealthy societies waste away. A nation's vigor depends on that of its citizens.

"Contemporary cities cannot meet contemporary needs unless they are adapted to new conditions. Large cities govern the life of the nation. If large cities are stifled, the nation will founder!

"To transform cities, we must discover the basic principles of contemporary urban planning." (6, p. 78)

Le Corbusier's theory of urban planning, as it developed over the following decades, is a search for these basic principles. In the interest of clarity it may be divided into four stages:

1. A CONTEMPORARY CITY   1922
2. THE RADIANT CITY   1935
3. THE GREAT WASTE   1937
4. REGIONAL PLANNING   1939

1. A CONTEMPORARY CITY   1922

Le Corbusier's principles of urban planning, as presented in the *L'Esprit nouveau* articles republished in 1925 in his book *Urbanisme (The City of Tomorrow and its Planning)*, proceed from a project for "A Contemporary City for Three Million People," which he presented at the 1922 Salon d'Automne. Feeling that his project had been misunderstood, he described it in a 1925 *L'Esprit nouveau* article. As he explains:

"It was greeted with considerable astonishment . . . arousing anger in some and enthusiasm in others. My proposed solution was radical, uncompromising. There was no written explanation of the plans, and, unfortunately, not everyone is capable of reading plans. I should have been there to answer the kind of questions that spring from deep human feelings. Such questions

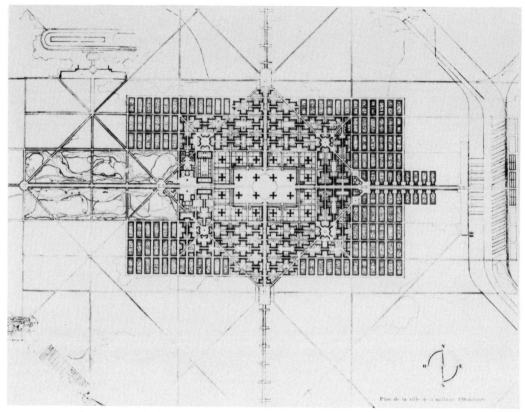

Plate 20: Plan of a contemporary city for 3 million people.

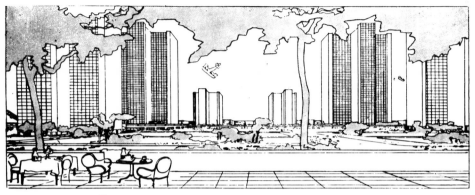

Plate 21: Perspective view of the "contemporary city."

are of major importance and should not be left unanswered." (6, p. 157)

Le Corbusier's "contemporary city" has three basic components: a central business district surrounded by residential districts; a large, open belt for future expansion; and, farther off, suburbs with residential and industrial areas. The business district can accommodate from 400,000 to 600,000 people with a density of 1,200 persons per acre. The surrounding residential districts have 600,000 residents with 120 persons per acre. There are two kinds of apartment buildings: some, built around parks, form large, closed city blocks; others, consisting of long slabs placed at right angles to each other, form an irregular open pattern. These slabs, set in large planted areas, straddle the streets. Two million people live in garden-cities located in the suburbs. The city itself is densely populated, since:

"The higher the density of a city's population, the shorter the distances to be covered. . . . However, though we must increase the density of the population, we must also greatly increase planted areas. . . . We must therefore build the city *vertically*." (6, p. 160)

Le Corbusier developed four basic principles:

"(1) *Relieve the congestion of central districts* to satisfy traffic requirements.
"(2) *Increase the population density of central districts* to facilitate business contacts.
"(3) *Improve traffic flow.* This means that we shall have to change totally the

Office buildings.

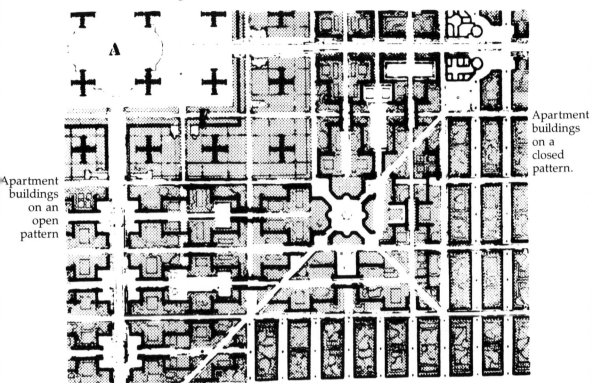

Apartment buildings on an open pattern

Apartment buildings on a closed pattern.

Plate 22: Detail of the "contemporary city" plan.

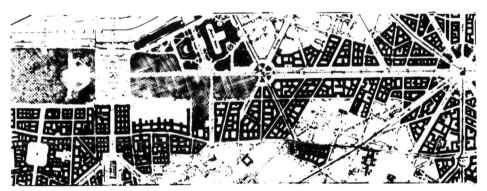

Plate 23: Plan of the Champs-Elysées area of Paris *drawn at the same scale*.

existing concept of a street, which is outdated by contemporary means of transportation: subways, cars, streetcars, airplanes.

"(4) *Increase planted areas.* This is the only way to promote healthy conditions and create a tranquil atmosphere that will offset the strain produced by the accelerated tempo of modern business." (6, p. 92)

Le Corbusier, returning to the problem of city streets, remarked:

"Existing streets are old dirt roads that have been paved over with subways underneath.

"Modern streets will form a new organism: a sort of elongated workshop or warehouse where delicate and complex utility services can be easily installed and maintained. These services must be accessible at every point." (6, p. 160)

He proposed that three kinds of streets be placed one above the other:

"(a) There will be underground streets for trucks. If, in some districts, buildings were raised on stilts, these streets would not be underground.
"(b) At the ground-floor level of the buildings, there will be a complex network of regular streets that will allow local traffic to reach all parts of the city.
"(c) *Big elevated highways* 40 or 60 meters (130 or 200 ft.) wide, which are made of reinforced concrete, will run on the North-South and East-West axes of the city for rapid *through traffic*. They will be connected to the local streets by ramps at 800- or 1,200-meter (½ or ¾ of a mile) intervals.
"The number of existing streets *must be reduced by two-thirds.*" (6, p. 161)

Le Corbusier's proposed street system, based on a 400-meter (¼ of a mile) grid sometimes divided in half, was determined by appropriate distances between subway stations or bus stops as well as by acceptable walking distances for pedestrians. He also stressed the need for planted areas:

"The new spirit of architecture and the emerging art of urban planning can satisfy our deepest needs by bringing nature into the city landscape. . . ." (6, p. 71)

"Apartment buildings will be twenty, forty, sixty stories high. But men, who remain 1.75 meters (5 ft. 9 in.) tall, will feel ill at ease when they walk down the streets, surrounded by these giant constructions. We must bridge the painful gap between man and his city by introducing a mean that fits into both scales. . . . *We must plant trees!*" (6, p. 70)

Le Corbusier subsequently complained that his project was interpreted as a utopian dream:

"In 1922, when I drew up plans for a *contemporary* city for 3 million people, all the critics, without exception, started talking about my city of the future! My protests had no effect. I insist that I know nothing about the future, that I know only about the present. People respond with a sly evasion, 'You are concerned with the future,' which implies that 'they' (everyone else) are concerned with the present. It's a lie! As a humble seeker, I live in the present, in the world as it exists today, while they live in, and off, the past." (11, p. 180)

He did, however, stress that his project was conceived as a diagram:

"Proceeding like a chemist in his laboratory, I dismissed special cases or accidental instances and assumed an ideal situation. I was not trying to overcome an existing state of things, *but to construct a rigorous, theoretical scheme that would make it possible to formulate the basic principles of contemporary urban planning.*

"For to plan a large contemporary city is to engage in a tremendous battle. And how can you fight a battle if you do not know exactly what you are fighting for?

"We must have guidelines. We must have basic principles of modern urban planning." (6, p. 158)

Le Corbusier formulated another general principle already mentioned in Chapter II: we should aim for diversity in the overall appearance of a city and unity in the individual buildings:

"When we walk through a city, our minds can evaluate the general plan and appreciate coordinated and majestic layouts. But our eye, limited to the narrower range of its visual field, sees only a succession of cells: a jagged, disjointed, diversified, complex, oppressive sight. . . . Overburdened, its only feeling is one of pain and fatigue, and the mind, after this initial defeat, is too harassed, exhausted, to respond to the splendid layouts."

He concluded:

"If these eclectic cells were based on a common standard, the impression of disorder would disappear, giving way to one of order and tranquility. If there were unity in the details, the mind, freed of encumbrances, would be able to appreciate the grandeur of the whole.

"The exact and ideal concept, already anticipated at the time of Louis XIV by Abbé Laugier, is as follows:

"(1) *Chaos and turmoil in the general plan* (meaning a composition full of contrasting elements—as in a fugue or symphony).

"(2) *Uniformity in the details* (meaning decency, restraint, and conformity in the details)." (6, p. 64)

Le Corbusier's second point has a further practical advantage:

"If we are to industrialize construction methods, we can no longer construct individual, custom-made buildings, each having its own peculiarities; we must build entire streets, entire districts. We must therefore study closely the basic unit, a human dwelling, and determine the right module and mass-produce it. The regular and quiet pattern formed by a succession of these units would then extend, far beyond the miserable corridor-street, to vast architectural compositions. Urban planning must do away with existing corridor-streets and, by designing new building developments, create a new architectural symphony on a much larger scale.

"The corridor-street and its two sidewalks, squeezed in between tall buildings, must go." (6, p. 68)

This first attack on the "corridor-street" was the onset of a campaign, pursued over many years, that forms an important part of his theory of urban planning.

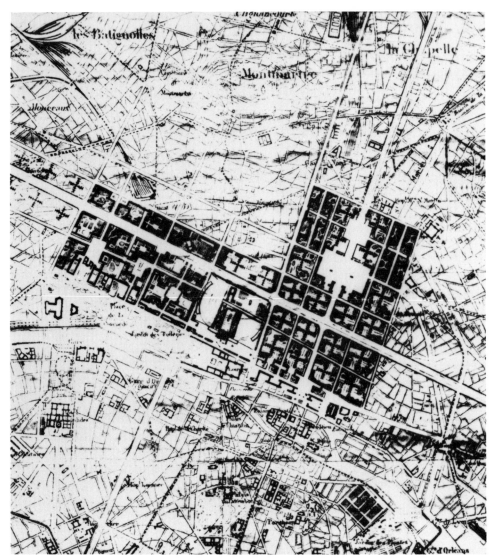

Plate 24: The "Plan Voisin" for Paris.

Plate 25: Perspective view of the "Plan Voisin."

The "Plan Voisin" For Paris

In the 1925 "Plan Voisin de Paris," financed in part by the Voisin motor company, Le Corbusier for the first time applied certain principles of his "contemporary city" to an existing situation: a partial renovation of Paris. The plan was, and still is, severely criticized. We must, however, realize that this, too, was intended as a diagram:

"The Plan Voisin does not claim to offer a detailed solution of the problems confronting this central district of Paris. But it may serve to bring our consideration of these problems into line with contemporary needs and set them in the right perspective. Its principles cut through the tangle of petty reforms with which day by day we delude ourselves." (6, p. 273)

The plan covers an area about two miles long, which lies north of the Rue de Rivoli and is divided into a business district in the East and a residential district in the West. All of the historical buildings are preserved.*

Le Corbusier, in the fourteenth chapter of *Urbanisme*, asks whether surgery or medicine should be applied to the ailing city of Paris. His radical "Plan Voisin" is clearly a surgical operation, justified by the gravity of the disease:

*In 1937, Le Corbusier drew another plan for the center of Paris that covers a much smaller area.

"The Old Paris committee has convened. We are glad to know that vandalism is being curbed. Of course, of course! We are reassured to learn that beauty is considered a legitimate need of citizens.

". . . But a person who is dying of heart and lung diseases does not do finger exercises on the harpsichord." (6, p. 245)

The Ciam and the Athens Charter

The formation of the CIAM (International Congress on Modern Architecture) in 1928 provided a mouthpiece for Le Corbusier's ideas on urban planning. During the 1933 meeting of the Congress, which was held in Athens, a charter was drawn up demanding a basic reform of urban planning.* While this restates most of the principles embodied in Le Corbusier's "Contemporary City" project, those listed under the headings of "Administration" and "Housing" anticipate the subsequent evolution of his thinking. First, urban planning should go beyond the city limits:

"Cities, like villages, must be studied in the context of their regional economies. City plans must give way to regional plans."

Second, city housing must be not only efficient but also pleasant:

"The best sites will be used for residential districts. Each room in an apartment will have sunlight during a minimum number of hours. . . ." (14, p. 30)

Since Le Corbusier here, as in his Paris renovation project, discusses such problems as financing and land expropriation, it is worth quoting his speech to the 1930 meeting of the CIAM in Brussels:

"Contemporary architecture and, still more, urban planning are closely connected with social problems. We should keep abreast of these developments through our own investigations, but I strongly urge that we steer clear of political and social problems in our meetings. They are extremely complex and, moreover, raise further economic problems. We are not qualified to discuss these difficult subjects.

"I repeat we must here confine ourselves to our role of architects and urban planners and, on this professional footing, inform those concerned about the possibilities offered by contemporary techniques and of the need for a new approach to architecture and urban planning." (11, p. 37)

2. THE RADIANT CITY   1935

The main difference between Le Corbusier's "radiant" and "contemporary" cities stems from his growing determination to give city dwellers a more pleasant as well as more efficient environment. This new concept was preceded by many years of anxiety and doubt. As he explains:

---

*The charter was not published until 1941. By then Le Corbusier had already set forth its basic principles in his "Pavillon des Temps Nouveaux" at the Paris exhibition of 1937.

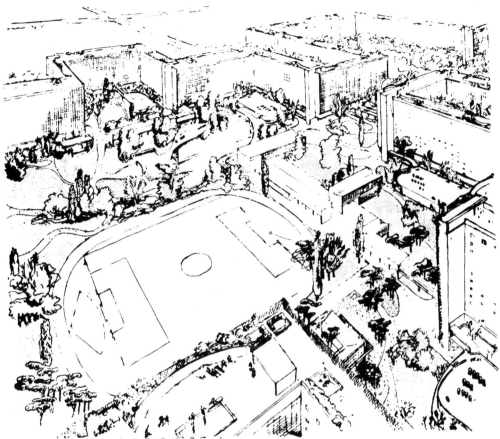

Plate: 26: The Radiant City. Perspective view.

"This takes me back to 1922 and the state of mind I was in while designing a *contemporary city for 3 million people.* My analyses, my calculations, and a powerful intuition had convinced me that I must set up *a new scale for the city.* . . . But how disturbed I was by the results! What anguished weeks I lived through! . . . I was tortured by the thought that the great empty spaces of this imaginary city, everywhere dominated by the sky, would be so dead, so dull, that its inhabitants would be panic-stricken.

"It took me eight anxious years to discover the solution.* It proceeded from the following question: what kind of a life should a machine age man really lead? How can I fill every moment of his daily life and, better, make these moments enjoyable? Still better, give this man a sense of personal freedom in this collective organism and the means of satisfying the personal initiatives resulting from this freedom?" (11, p. 105)

Le Corbusier's answer was suggested by the following idea:

"With these questions clearly formulated in my mind, I one day told myself: *sports must be an everyday activity,* and THEY MUST TAKE PLACE RIGHT

---

*The studies leading up to the principles of the "Radiant City" include seventeen plates drawn up in 1930.

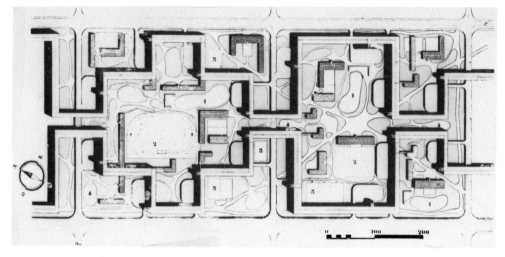

Plate 27: The Radiant City—Plan of a residential district.
1 swimming pools,   3 tennis courts,
2 stadium, soccer, etc.,   4 playgrounds.
The hatched and dotted areas indicate nurseries,
kindergartens, and schools.

OUTSIDE THE HOUSES. It seems a dizzyingly reckless proposition. And yet, once this idea was firmly anchored in my head, I was able to seek out stubbornly—and find—an answer. After studying the problem for a number of years, I arrived at the idea of the Radiant City. Sports grounds were right outside the houses." (11, p. 65)

Le Corbusier defines the goal of the "Radiant City" as follows:

"The radiant city, inspired by physical and human laws, proposes to bring machine age man *essential pleasures* . . .
    Sun in the house,
    a view of the sky through large windows,
    trees he can see from his house.
I say that the materials of urban design are:
    sun
    sky
    trees
    steel
    cement
in this order of importance."

Thinking of his "sports grounds right outside the houses," he adds:

"But we must not forget another source of happiness: a chance to participate actively in common pursuits that will benefit the whole community and alleviate the misery of less fortunate members." (11, pp. 85 and 86)

With this goal in mind, Le Corbusier greatly extended the ideas he had formulated for his "contemporary city." To begin with, he increased the density of the residential areas and completely eliminated the suburban garden-cities:

"The authorities want to force us to live in suburban garden-cities (60 to 120 residents per acre). . . . I propose to turn the city back into itself, enclose it within its own limits, and raise its population level to 400 residents per acre. We must eliminate garden-cities, with their spuriously natural surroundings. This will solve *the transport crisis.* And we must turn the dull-witted, retrograde, and suffocating city of Paris into a *green city, a radiant city. We must bring nature inside the walls of Paris;* it will be no more, nor less, contrived than that of garden-cities, but it will be much more useful." (11, p. 107)

The "radiant city," despite its higher density, frees considerably more ground space for pedestrians by raising all the buildings on stilts. By eliminating all closed city blocks and using only open building patterns, which straddle streets, it does away with conventional corridor-streets and also produces more attractive and varied open spaces:

"We have, needless to say, eliminated corridor-streets, now prevalent in all parts of the world. *Our apartment buildings have nothing to do with streets.* We have, moreover (and in perfectly good faith), completely reversed the present policy of urban planners, who want to make pedestrians run about *in the air* on elevated footbridges and let cars drive on the ground. *We have given* THE ENTIRE GROUND SURFACE *of the city over to pedestrians.* . . . And since our apartment buildings are raised on stilts, they can walk from one end of the city to the other in all directions. I add: NO PEDESTRIAN WILL EVER, UNDER ANY CIRCUMSTANCES, MEET A CAR!" (11, p. 108)

The different means of transportation will be organized as follows: cars will use elevated drives; trucks and streetcar routes will be located side by side under these drives, with underpasses for pedestrians.

The concentration of large numbers of people in tall apartment buildings will simplify their access to these buildings. As Le Corbusier explains, "2,700 people will use the same entrance."

"Cars will leave the elevated drive (which is a continuous stream of traffic) and enter an elevated car port in front of the main entrance. Instead of seventy-five doors opening onto the street, *there is only one door, and it is far away from the street.* . . . There will be a garage beneath the car port for the cars of building residents.*

"An entrance at ground level will be used by pedestrians. . . . This leads to a flexible network of octagonal and diagonal paths. . . . A sort of continuous marquee runs down the center of each path . . . : the pedestrian's umbrella."

Underpasses at 400-meter (¼ of a mile) intervals will permit pedestrians to walk under the truck and streetcar routes. Streetcars will stop at every underpass. This plan allows for a convenient utility system:

"Utilities, placed under the slabs of the elevated drives, will be easy to

---

*One would assume that truck deliveries would be made at ground level.

get at and repair. At last! Or else they will be placed in trenches dug underneath the marquees of the pedestrian paths, where they will be protected from rain and easily accessible." (11, p. 124)

Le Corbusier concludes:

"Here, then, the 'artificial garden-city' is an effective concept: *because the city is vertical, not horizontal.* Height resolves every difficulty.

"And the city immediately becomes an organized entity: transportation problems are solved; common services, which eliminate waste, bring urgently needed time-saving benefits to each household."* (11, p. 57)

Le Corbusier later used the ideas expressed in his "Radiant City" for a number of specific urban planning projects:

"These purely theoretical ideas have made it possible to formulate basic principles in ideal terms, above the battleground. Can such a theory be lifted out of its utopian framework and applied to concrete situations? Once a theory has led you to the heart of a problem, you acquire certitudes, guidelines, and are able to study particular cases in the light of a basic postulate. . . . In the years that followed, the principles embodied in the Radiant City directly confronted concrete realities in my plans for Algiers, Stockholm, Barcelona, Nemours, etc., etc." (11, p. 156)

3. THE GREAT WASTE   1937

In his "Radiant City" Le Corbusier had already eliminated suburban garden-cities. Going one step further, he now proposes to eliminate all suburbs on the grounds that they waste time and money. This development, a consequence of his trip to the United States, is described in a chapter of his book, *Quand les cathédrales étaient blanches (When Cathedrals Were White)*, entitled "Le Grand Gaspillage," "the great waste."

"I had for many years studied the harmful effects of that monstrous and disruptive outgrowth of our times: urban sprawl. It is easier to diagnose the illness in the U.S.A., where it exists on a larger scale and is a more desperate case." (13, p. 226)

He here analyzes the problem:

"My main argument in attempting to win over the American people to my reform of architecture and reorganization of the city is that our solar day has been misused. . . .

"The proper equilibrium of this twenty-four-hour cycle must be discovered and restored. This is our only possible salvation!

"I express our solar day as it exists now in the U.S.A. and also Europe by a circle (Fig. 62). The first segment (A) represents sleep . . . (B) is an hour and a half wasted in transportation—subways, trains, buses, streetcars. (C) is the eight-hour working day we now devote to necessary manufactured

---

*Le Corbusier also advocated a sweeping agricultural reform described as the "Radiant Farm" and "Radiant Village." (11, pp. 319–337)

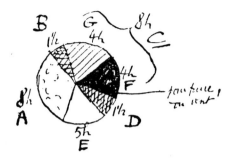

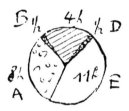

Fig. 63

articles; (D) is, once more, time wasted in transportation. This leaves us (E), five leisure hours in the evening." (13, p. 252)

Indeed, in addition to the hours lost in trains, subways, buses, etc., we must count those lost in constructing, maintaining, and operating transport systems as well as in extending utilities to the suburbs. Le Corbusier estimates that we each pay for this every day with four hours of additional work.

Le Corbusier here points out:

"The hours lost in reaching our different workingplaces *are nothing compared* with the daily work hours lost in paying for this unhappy situation." (13, p. 282)

"Socially useful manufactured articles are shoes, clothes, food and drink, housing (and, more generally, shelter), books, movies, plays, works of art. The rest is mere wind, but it has created a devastating hurricane: *the great waste.*

"The verdict is clear. Let us draw the necessary conclusions and reschedule our time accordingly: which is to say, reconstruct our cities and revitalize the countryside.

". . . A modern city should have no suburbs. Modern techniques allow us to recover in height what we lose in breadth. The city should be concen-

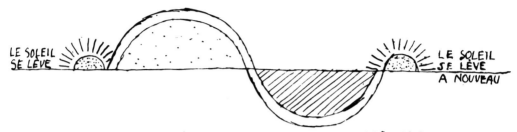

LA JOURNÉE SOLAIRE DE 24 HEURES EST
LA MESURE DE TOUTES LES ENTREPRISES
URBANISTIQUES

Urban planning should always be based on the twenty-four-hour solar day.

Fig. 64

trated, compact. The problem of transportation would then resolve itself. We would rediscover our feet. . . .

"I am drawing another 24-hour solar-day circle (Fig. 63); there are eight hours for sleep (A); half an hour for transportation (B); four hours for productive work, which are all that will be needed (C); another half hour for transportation (D). This leaves us eleven daily leisure hours (E).

"America's *great waste* allowed me to get to the bottom of our unhappy situation and see it more clearly than was possible in Europe, which has the same disease. *And I now realize that my two solar-day circles simply refer to the past and to the future.*" (13, pp. 258 and 259)

Le Corbusier's famous diagram of the solar day is his illustration of the twenty-four-hour unit on which urban planning should be based (Fig. 64):

4. REGIONAL PLANNING 1939

During World War II Le Corbusier used his enforced leisure to expand his urban planning theories to a regional scale. His idea of the city was by then firmly established, and it was time for him to move on.

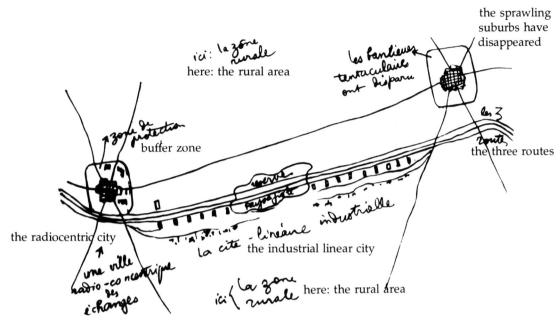

here: the rural area

ici: la zone rurale

the sprawling
suburbs have
disappeared

les banlieues tentaculaires ont disparu

zone de protection
buffer zone

les 3 routes
the three routes

réserve

the radiocentric city

une ville radio-concentrique des échanges

La cité-linéaire industrielle
the industrial linear city

ici { la zone rurale here: the rural area

Fig. 65

The Four Routes

Le Corbusier's urban planning studies proceeded from the recent "revolutions" in social conditions and building techniques; his regional planning studies, from a similar "revolution" in transport systems or, as he calls them, "the four routes": roads, waterways (in France this would include canals), railways, and airlines.

"What was the reason for the birth of this new field of study? The radical transformation, in less than a century, of the great routes along which men live: roads, waterways, railways, and airlines. Machines, breaking through millennia of history, replaced the *traditional speed* of men on foot or horseback by *the twenty or a hundred times faster* speeds of railroads, cars, steamers, and planes. Speed has transformed the values of space and time and, in so doing, has created tremendous misery."

Le Corbusier proposed to examine the practical consequences of this problem in his book *Sur les quatre routes,* published in 1941 but written two years earlier:

"I wrote it in the fall of 1939 during the first three months of war. It anticipated victory and set forth a partial program for the great building

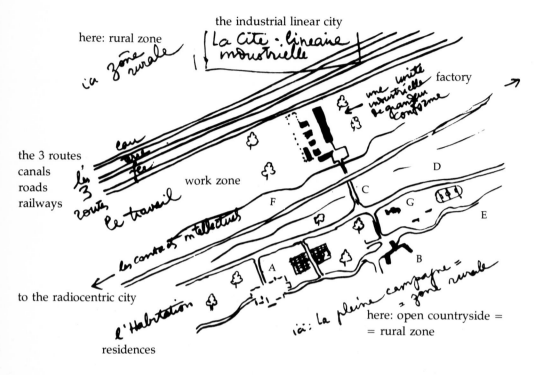

the industrial linear city

here: rural zone

factory

the 3 routes
canals
roads
railways

work zone

to the radiocentric city

here: open countryside =
= rural zone

residences

Fig. 66

enterprises that would soon have been required. It will be published, with no changes, after the defeat, for a defeat, in the course of human events, means only that a chance has been replaced by a mischance." (16, p. 8)

Despite the broader view suggested here, *Sur les quatre routes* consists primarily of urban planning principles that Le Corbusier had developed in his "contemporary" and "radiant" cities. It does, however, make the following point: regional, even more than urban, planning requires architects to work with other specialists.

"The four routes require teamwork, and the team must cover the whole spectrum of needed specialists. . . .

"Architecture, in confronting the four routes, faces a task of unlimited scope. A single individual would never get to the bottom of it, for omniscience and omnipotence are not prerogatives of mortal men. Builders, like scientists and technicians, must consequently resort to specialization.

"On the four routes described in this program architects will have to work closely with engineers. Tomorrow's tasks require builders."

Le Corbusier nonetheless gives the key role to the architect:

"In the command posts and central offices, he will be the coordinator, the conciliator, the *harmonizer*. As such, he will discover and integrate different factors. . . .

"The architectural profession will be opened wide." (17, pp. 27–29)

The Industrial Linear City

During World War II Le Corbusier participated in a study group called AS-CORAL (Assembly of builders for an architectural revolution), which was concerned with planning and building on a regional scale. A small book published in 1945, *Les Trois établissements humains (The Three Human Establishments)**, presented the results of these studies.

Le Corbusier identifies three basic "human establishments"—agricultural, industrial, and commercial—and argues that their respective forms and locations should be adapted to present-day needs:

"We thus propose, for farm reform, a new or revised form of *agriculture.* . . . For industry, a form that will specifically satisfy its requirements: *industrial linear cities. . . . Radiocentric cities,* situated at the intersection of major highways . . . , will again become commercial, intellectual, administrative, and governmental centers" (Fig. 65). (21, p.72)

Le Corbusier had already proposed a "Radiant Farm," in *La Ville radieuse*, and his "radiocentric city" adds little, beyond the name, to his existing urban projects; but the "industrial linear city," as he emphasizes, is a new concept. Most modern cities, he points out, grew up at the points of intersection of important trade routes. These "radiocentric cities," which are well adapted to the exchange of goods or of ideas, are ill adapted to the needs of modern industry: namely, the transport of raw materials and manufactured products. Industrial cities should, instead, stretch out *along* appropriate transport routes:

"Lined up along these routes, they will naturally take the form of 'linear cities.' The linear city thus follows a trail inscribed in a country's geography. It is based on the principle of alignment, not dispersion. . . . " (21, p. 102)

Factories scattered throughout the countryside, as proposed during the prewar period, not only would spoil these regions but also would be inefficient.

Le Corbusier analyzes the functioning of the "linear city" as carefully as he had analyzed that of the "radiant city." The key to the whole system lies in the three transport routes that bring raw materials and distribute manufactured products: waterways, roads, and railroads. These will run along one side of the factory. Overhead conveyors will carry shipments to and from the factory. The typical site plan is as follows (Fig. 66):

(A) Houses. (B) Apartment building. (C) Road to the factory. (D) Road connecting dwellings and common services. (E) Pedestrian paths. (F) Green buffer zone and parkway leading to radiocentric cities. (G) Common services: nurseries, schools, movies, libraries, youth centers, sport facilities, etc.

In addition to the linear city's green zone between the factories and the worker's dwellings, Le Corbusier provides a large green zone between the industrial linear city and the radiocentric cities. His earlier urban projects had envisaged such a zone as a way of protecting residential cities from industrial areas. He now, however, sees it as a safety valve or buffer zone that will soften the impact of their colliding energies. It is a place where people from both cities will be able to meet. Laboratories, libraries, various research fa-

---

*The book was written by Le Corbusier and nine other members of ASCORAL. The passages quoted here are taken from chapters written by Le Corbusier.

cilities, and certain universities will be located there. Big sporting events will take place there.

Le Corbusier attached particular importance to his idea of the industrial linear city. Returning to the subject in a small book *Mise au point (Explanations)*, written in 1965, he says:

"By studying the single problem of equipping a machine age civilization in every kind of country and climate, I realized (with the same sort of astonishment one might feel on suddenly seeing a flying saucer or a Sputnik) that our machine age society has no industrial establishment, no industrial cities; and that this third new human establishment, the 'Industrial Linear City' . . . solves problems that preoccupy all reformers who are men of goodwill, whatever their political affiliations." (37, p. 39)

CHAPTER VIII
The Reasons Behind Le Corbusier's Ideas

I N 1925 LE CORBUSIER published a book on, and relentless criticism of, *L'Art décoratif d'aujourd'hui (Decorative Art Today)* which, like his first books on architecture and urban planning, consisted mainly of articles previously published in *L'Esprit nouveau*. At the end of the book he added a "confession," which he explains as follows:

"A friend who had closely followed the development of the idea of this book in my *L'Esprit nouveau* articles and was also acquainted with my background told me: 'The only thing people know about you are buildings completely stripped of decoration. They will think: this man does not see the beauty of little flowers; he does not hear the music of the great god Pan, animating all of nature. He feeds on theories; his heart is arid. You cannot let your principles, fruits of a long odyssey through the archipelagoes of human knowledge, be judged in such a summary way. You should let people know about the doubts and the enthusiasms that you experienced during the past twenty-five years, the very years when our era, in a final spurt of its long evolution, seemed to be finding its shape. You should explain the reasons behind your ideas by explaining yourself. You owe your readers a . . . *confession.*

"Here is the confession."

It begins in 1900, when Le Corbusier, aged thirteen, entered the Art School in his native La-Chaux-de-Fonds:

"Twenty-five years ago, as a boy, I decided to study art. Though I have ended up as an architect, it was after passing through this prior phase of art, which seemed to offer greater freedom, closer contact with nature and more immediate emotions. Under the pressure of the conquering hero spirit of the times, I jumped to the conclusion that only decorative art could lead to serious work; the fine arts seemed too capricious.

"My teacher, an excellent instructor, was an outdoor man, and he turned his students into outdoor men. I spent my childhood with my friends outdoors. . . . I knew what flowers look like, outside and inside; I knew the shapes and colors of the birds; I understood how a tree grows and why it is able to stand upright, even in a storm.

"My teacher said: 'Nature alone is truthful; it can inspire man-made works. But do not treat nature as landscape painters do and show only its outward appearance. Search for the cause, the form, the animating spirit of things and synthesize this in the *ornaments* that you design.' For ten years we composed a sort of ode to our country.

"My teacher said: 'We are going to renovate houses and revive some of the beautiful old crafts.' All twenty of us chose our various vocations: stone sculpture, wood sculpture, ceramics, mosaics, glasswork, brass work, engraving, ironwork, jewelry, frescos, etc. What a crew! How gloriously high-spirited we were and how deeply committed to our faith!

". . . During these years art workshops were being founded. We decorated chapels and concert halls; we made furniture, jewelry, tombstones. Most of us were no longer living at home. We rented barns near town, where we slept at night in order to be closer to nature. It was REAL LIFE: a sense of exaltation in the midst of adolescent miseries.

"We founded a school (somewhat as the Weimar Bauhaus was to do ten years later). . . . Some of us went away to travel, one after the other. When we came back, we were stunned and disturbed by the ebullient faith still animating those who stayed behind." (5, pp. 197–200)

Le Corbusier, who was one of those who traveled, visited museums and libraries and occasionally worked for architects in various cities.

In 1908 he joined the firm of Auguste Perret in Paris and worked there, part-time, for over a year.

"Auguste Perret had just finished the Ponthieu Garage and his building in the rue Franklin. He told everyone, in martial tones: 'I work in reinforced concrete.' Indeed, it really was a battle. Those were heroic times, and Auguste Perret was the hero. He won a sure place for himself in architecture, which he will occupy for many years.

"Auguste Perret was surprised to see that I was fond of visiting museums. He used to say: 'If I had time, I would study mathematics; it develops the mind.'

"I studied mathematics, which later proved almost entirely useless, but it perhaps developed my mind.

"Auguste Perret also said: 'A construction must be perfect . . . ; ornament hides imperfections.' I became passionately interested in construction." (5, pp. 204–207)

"An accidental set of circumstances led me to Germany, where I traveled for over a year. I had been commissioned to study decorative art in Germany and was given a letter of introduction authorizing me to visit factories, commercial establishments, schools, and design workshops. I visited everything and asked questions about everything I saw. . . . I saw an abominable machine at work in ornamental metal workshops: a hammering machine. Flawlessly smooth iron sections were fed into the machine; in a few seconds, it completely covered them with bumps so that they looked like pieces of old scrap iron." (5, p. 209)

"This third chapter of my life set me wandering again in search of enlightenment, trying to understand the origins, principles, and uses of art. I saw the Paris, Vienna, Berlin, and Munich styles, and they all seemed questionable. But I knew that reinforced concrete and steel demanded special forms, which would be altogether new. I was much disturbed by the arbitrary character of current design.

"I then set out on a long and, as it turned out, decisive journey through the cities and countrysides of reputedly unspoiled countries. From Prague I went down the Danube, visiting Serbia, Rumania, Bulgaria, and Turkey, where I saw Andrinopolos [Edirne], the sea of Marmara, Istanbul, and Bursa.

"I saw the human spirit's great eternal monuments. I succumbed, above all, to the irresistible attraction of the Mediterranean. It was not too soon, after ten years of German decorative art and architecture (heavily publicized in journals).

"I saw the Turkish architecture of Adrianople, the Byzantine architecture of Istanbul and Salonica, the Persian architecture of Bursa. I saw the Parthenon, Pompeii, and the Coliseum. I saw what architecture was: the magnificent play of forms in light, a coherent intellectual system. For architecture has nothing to do with decoration. It exists in the complex and stately monuments handed down by past civilizations, but it *also exists in the humblest dwellings*, for example, a garden wall; it exists in any building, great or small, whose geometry creates a mathematical proportion.

"With my knapsack on my back, free to follow every unexpected turning of the way, I traveled through these countries on foot, on horseback, by boat, by car, like a pilgrim. After this yearlong journey where, within all these different civilizations, I saw a unifying human principle at work, I was convinced that a new century, the twentieth century, had emerged. . . .

"But the public was no longer able to judge things rightly; bric-a-brac, vulgarity, and pretentiousness had become the order of the day. Nobody knew what to do. . . . I thought that we should not react but rather act. For simplification had become a vital need; since we did not wish to perish, our instinct for survival would in itself restore our sense of what is healthy, and therefore beautiful." (5, pp. 210–214)

115

"I was left with this conviction: We have to begin from scratch. We have to formulate the problem. A man swept up in life's whirlwind is carried beyond esthetics. Between his twentieth and thirtieth years he rounds the cape. The fundamental drives that will shape his life are then at work. He chooses his life, without realizing he has done so, without time to ask himself should I go here? or there? In his thirtieth year he finds himself in a certain place, having rounded, or not rounded, the cape.

"It looked like a bog.

"*I found myself* working in industry, in a factory with machines, production schedules, cost analyses, payment deadlines, balance sheets. This was it! After the war, when everyone dreamed of organizing and creating, I ran a technical research bureau.

". . . During these long hardworking years I became attuned to the true spirit of our age. This spirit, which is the animating principle of a working society, is the how and why of social phenomena. . . . It gives artists a sense of purpose." (5, p. 217)

"I had met Ozenfant, a lucid man, in 1918. France was then recovering from the war. We believed that a steel age had begun, that our previous years of anxiety, confusion, and experimentation would now be followed by a period of construction.

"In 1920, together with Paul Dermée, we founded *L'Esprit nouveau, an international journal of contemporary activities.* We wanted to stop questioning and start building, to wrest each day a new certainty from our studies and add it to that cycle of human certainties where ideas are born, develop—and, as we were well aware, die.

". . . With resolute minds and hearts that were not sequestered in an ivory tower, we tried to seize the moment and express its meaning." (5, p. 217)

◣◥

Le Corbusier's 1925 "confession" looks back at the earlier development of his ideas. *Mise au point (Explanations),* written in 1965, a month before he died, looks forward to their future destiny. He is still aware that new ideas, which arise out of new conditions, must change as these conditions change. But he is now also aware of the fatal time gap between the birth and application of ideas.

"It takes at least twenty years for an idea to be recognized, thirty for it be appreciated, and fifty for it to be applied, when it should, by then, be changing. . . .

"I, for my part, spent fifty years studying housing. . . . I should not have been able to carry out this enterprise had it not been for the wonderful support of the young people who worked in my office at 35 rue de Sèvres, their passion, their faith, their probity. I thank them all. Some fertile seeds have probably been planted among them. In later years they will perhaps think of old Corbu, who now tells them: 'We must work according to the dictates of our consciences. . . . This is where the human drama is acted out. . . .' "

Le Corbusier here quotes a letter from one of his former assistants, asking: "Corbu's ideas will one day spread through the whole world but when? . . ." And he reflects:

"Yes, nothing can be handed on except ideas, which are the noblest fruits of human labor. Such ideas may, or may not, prevail over death, perhaps in some unforeseeable new form." (37, pp. 48–60)

Bibliography

1. **Etude sur le mouvement d'art décoratif en Allemagne.**
   Published under the name of Ch.-E. Jeanneret, La Chaux–de-Fonds: Haefeli & Cie., 1912.
   Reprint. New York: Da Capo Press, 1968.

2. **Après le cubisme.**
   Published under the names of Ozenfant and Jeanneret, Paris: Editions des Commentaires, 1918.

3. **Vers une architecture.**
   Paris: G. Crès, 1923.
   Reprint. Paris: Vincent, Fréal & Cie., 1958.
   Reprint. Paris: Arthaud, 1977.
   Translated into English under the title "Towards a New Architecture" by Frederick Etchells, New York: Warren and Putnam and London: Rodker, 1927.
   Reprint in English, London: The Architectural Press, 1946.
   Reprint in English, New York: Praeger Publishers, 1960.
   Translated into German under the title "Kommende Baukunst" by Hans Hildebrand, Stuttgart: 1926.
   Reprint in German under the title "Ausblick auf eine Architektur," Berlin: Verlag Ullstein, 1963.
   Translated into Italian by P. Cerri, P. Nicoline and C. Fiorini, Milan: Editione Longanesi, 1973.
   Translated into Spanish under the title "Hacia una Architectura" by J.M. Alinari, Buenos Aires: Poseidon, 1964.
   Translated into Portugese: Editoria Perspectiva, 1973.
   Translated into Serbo-Croatian: Gradjevinska Kujiga, 1974.
   Translated in Hungarian: Corina, 1977.

4. **La Peinture moderne.**
   Published under the names of Ozenfant and Jeanneret, Paris: G. Crès, 1925.

5. **L'Art décoratif d'aujourd'hui.**
   Paris: G. Crès, 1925.
   Reprint. Paris: Vincent, Fréal & Cie., 1959.

Reprint. Paris: Arthaud, 1978.
Translated into Italian by Manuel Co-
cever and Nelly Mazzocoli Rettmeyer,
Bari: Laterza, 1972 and 1973.

6. **Urbanisme.**
Paris: G. Crès, 1925
Reprint. Paris: Vincent, Fréal & Cie.,
1966.
Reprint. Paris: Arthaud, 1977 and
1980.
Translated into English under the title
"The City of Tomorrow and Its Plan-
ning" by Frederick Etchells, New
York: Payson and Clark and London:
John Rodker: 1929.
Reprint in English, London: The Ar-
chitectural Press, 1947.
Reprint in English, Cambridge, Mass.:
MIT Press, 1971.
Translated into German under the title
"Städtebau" by Hans Hildebrand,
Stuttgart: Deutsche Verlagsanstalt,
1929.
Reprint in German: Deutsche Verlag-
sanstalt, 1979.
Translated into Italian: Nicola Zani-
chelle, 1979.
Translated into Spanish: Ediciones In-
finito, 1958.
Translated into Castilian: Poseidon,
1979.

7. **Almanach d'architecture moderne.**
Paris: G. Crès, 1926.
Translated into Japanese: Kajima In-
stitute, 1979.

8. **Une Maison—un palais.**
Paris: G. Crès, 1928.
Reprint: Bottega d'Erasmo, 1976.
Translated into Japanese: Kajima In-
stitute, 1978.

9. **Précisions sur un état présent de
l'architecture et de l'urbanisme.**
Paris: G. Crès, 1930.
Reprint. Paris: Vincent, Fréal & Cie.,
1960.
Translated into German under the title
"Festellungen zu Architektur und
Städtebau" by H. Korssakof—
Schröder, Berlin: Verlag Ullstein, 1964.
Translated into Italian under the title
"Precisazioni sullo stato attuale dell'
architektura e dell' urbanistica" by
Francesco Tentori, Bari: Laterza, 1979.
Translated into Spanish: Poseidon.
Translated into Japanese: Kajima In-
stitute, 1979.

10. **Croisade ou le crépuscule des académies.**
Paris: G. Crès, 1932.

11. **La Ville radieuse.**
Paris: Editions de l'Architecture
d'Aujourd'hui, 1935.
Reprint. Paris: Vincent, Fréal & Cie.,
1964.
Translated into English under the title
"The Radiant City" by Pamela Knight,
Eleanor Levieux, and Derek Coltman,
New York: The Orion Press, 1967.

12. **Aircraft**
London: The New Vision, 1935.

13. **Quand les cathédrales étaient
blanches.**
Paris: Plon, 1937.
Reprint. Paris: Plon, 1965.
Pocketbook edition, Paris: Gonthier,
1965.
Reprint. Paris: Gonthier-Denoël, 1977.
Translated into English under the title
"When Cathedrals Were White" by
Francis E. Hyslop, New York: Reynal
and Hichcock, 1947.
Reprint. New York: Harcourt, Brace,
Jovanovich.
Reprint. New York: McGraw-Hill,
1965.
Translated into Spanish under the title
"Cuando las Catedrales eran blan-
cas," Buenos Aires: Poseidon, 1948.
Translated into Italian by Mario San-
giorgio: Faenza, 1975.

14. **Des Canons, des munitions? merci!
des logis . . . S.V.P.**
Paris: Editions de l'Architecture
d'Aujourd'hui, 1938.

15. **Le Lyrisme des temps nouveaux et
l'urbanisme.**
Colmar: Le Point, 1939.

16. **Destin de Paris.**
Paris: Sorlot, 1941.

17. **Sur les quatre routes.**
Paris: Gallimard, 1941.
Reprint. Paris: Gonthier-Denoël, 1969.
Translated into English under the title
"The Four Routes" by Dorothy Dodd,
London: Dobson, 1947.
Translated into Spanish: Gustavo Gili,
1971.
Translated into Japanese: Kajima In-
stitute, 1978.

18. **La Maison des hommes.**
In collaboration with François de Pierrefeu, Paris: Plon, 1942.
Translated into English by Clive Entwistle and Gordon Holt under the title "The Home of Man," London: The Architectural Press, 1949.
Translated into Swedish by Austin Grandjean, Stockholm: Bokförlaget Prisma, 1961.
Translated into Spanish by Miguel Perez Ferrero, Madrid: Espasa Calpe, 1945.
Reprint in Spanish, Buenos Aires: Poseidon, 1978 and 1979.
Translated into Danish: Stjerneborgerne vintens, 1967.
Translated into Japanese: Kajima Institute, 1976.

19. **Les Constructions Murondins.**
Paris: Chiron, 1942.

20. **Entretien avec les étudiants des écoles d'architecture.**
Paris: Denoël, 1943.
Reprint. Paris: Editions de Minuit, 1957.
Translated into Spanish by Nina de Kalada, Buenos Aires: Ediciones Infinito, 1959.
Translated into English by Pierre Chase under the title "Le Corbusier Talks with Students," New York: The Orion Press, 1961.
Translated in German: Rowohlt Verlag, 1960.

21. **Les Trois établissements humains.**
In collaboration with N. Bézard, J. Commelin, Coudoin, J. Dayre, H. Dubreuil, Leyritz, Hanning, Aujames, De Looze, Paris: Denoël, 1945.
Reprint. Paris: Editions de Minuit, 1959.
Translated into Spanish, Buenos Aires: Poseidon, 1959.
Translated into Italian: Editione di Communita, 1960.
Reprint in Italian: Etaskompas, 1966.
Translated into Portugese: Editoria Perspectiva, 1970.
Translated into Japanese: Kajima Institute, 1978.

22. **Propos d' urbanisme.**
Paris: Bousselier, 1946.
Translated into English by Clive Entwistle under the title "Concerning Town Planning," London: The Architectural Press, 1948.
Translated into German under the title "Grundfragen des Städtebaues" by Claudia and Eduard Neuenschwandler, Stuttgart: Hatze, 1945.
Translated into Italian by G. Bernabei, Bologna: Zanichelli, 1980.

23. **Manière de penser l' urbanisme.**
Paris: Editions de l'Architecture d'Aujourd'hui, 1946.
Reprint. Paris: Gonthier-Denoël, 1963 and 1977.
Translated into English under the title "Looking at City Planning" by Eleanor Levieux, New York: Grossman, 1971.
Translated into Spanish by E.L. Reval, Buenos Aires: Ediciones Infinito, 1959.
Translated into Japanese, 1952.
Translated into Italian under the title "Maniera di Pensare l' Urbanistica" by Giuseppe Scatore, Bari: Laterza, 1965.
Translated into German under the title "Von Sim und Unsim der Städte," Zurich: Benziger Verlag, 1974.
Translated into Portugese: Publicacoes Europa-America, 1964.
Translated into Swedish: Ab. Rabenet and Sjogren Bokforlag, 1966.
Translated into Hungarian: Gondolat.
Reprint in Portuguese: Editoria Perspectiva, 1969.
Translated into Serbo-Croatian: Gradjevinska Kujiga, 1970.

24. **United Nations Headquarters.**
New York: Reinhold, 1947.
Translated into Spanish by Miguel Diez Gonzales, Buenos Aires: Kraft, 1948.

25. **New World of Space.**
New York: Reynal and Hitchcock, 1948.

26. **Le Modulor.**
Paris: Editions de l'Architecture d'Aujourd'hui, 1950 and 1963.
Reprint. Paris: Gonthier-Denoël, 1977.
Translated into Japanese, Tokyo: Kokusai, Kentiku, Kyokai, 1952.
Translated into German by Richard Herre and J.G. Gotta'sche, Stuttgart: Buchhandlung Nachfolger, 1953.
Reprint in German: Deutsche Verlagsanstalt, 1977.

Translated into English under the title "The Modulor" by Peter de Francia and Anna Bostock, London: Faber and Cambridge, Mass,: Harvard University Press, 1954.
Reprint in English, Cambridge, Mass.: The MIT Press, 1968.
Translated into Spanish: Poseidon, 1959.
Translated into Bulgarian: Balgarski Boudojnik.
Translated into Italian (with "Modulor 2") under the title "Il Modulor e Modulor 2", Milan: Gabriele Mazotta, 1974.
Reprint in Japanese: Kajima Institute, 1977.

27. **Poésie sur Alger.**
Paris: Falaize, 1950.

28. **L'Unité d'habitation de Marseille.**
Mulhouse: Le Point, 1950.
Translated into English under the title "The Marseille Block" by Geoffrey Sainsbury, London: Harvill, 1953.
Translated into Italian: Libreria Eredi Virgilio Veshi, 1977.

29. **Une Petite maison**
Zurich: Girsberger, 1954. Zurich: Artémis.

30. **Modulor 2.**
Paris: Editions de l'Architecture d'Aujourd'hui, 1955.
Reprint. Paris: Gonthier-Denoël.
Translated into German by Richard Herre: Deutsche Verlagsanstalt, 1958.
Reprint in German, 1979.
Translated into English under the title "Modulor 2" by Peter de Francia and Anna Bostock, London: Faber, 1958, and Cambridge, Mass.: Harvard University Press, 1958.
Reprint in English, Cambridge, Mass.: The MIT Press, 1968.
Translated into Spanish: Poseidon, 1959.
Translated into Italian: Gabriele Mazotta, 1974.
Translated into Japanese: Kajima Institute, 1976.

31. **L'Urbanisme est une clef.**
Paris: Editions Forces Vives, 1955. Reprint, 1966.

32. **Les Plans de Paris 1956–1922.**
Paris: Editions de Minuit, 1956.

33. **Ronchamp.**
Zurich: Girsberger, 1957. Zurich: Artémis. Reprint, Stuttgart: Verlag Gerd Hatje, 1975.
Translated into German, Stuttgart: Verlag Gerd Hatje, 1957.
Translated into Italian, Milan: Edizioni di Comunita.
Translated into English under the title "The Chapel at Ronchamp," London: The Architectural Press, 1960.

34. **L'Atelier de la recherche patiente.**
Paris: Vincent, Fréal & Cie., 1960.
Translated into German under the title "Mein Werk," Stuttgart: Verlag Gerd Hatje, 1960.
Translated into English under the title "My Work," by James Palmes, New York: Praeger, 1960.
Translated into Italian under the title "La Mia Opera" by Maria Luisa Riccardi-Candiani, Torino: Boringhieri, 1961.

35. **Textes et dessins pour Ronchamp.**
Paris: Editions Forces Vives, 1965.

36. **Le Voyage d'Orient.**
Paris: Editions Forces Vives, 1966.
Translated into Italian under the title "Il Viaggio d'Oriente" by Tobia Bassanelli, Faenza: Faenza Editrice, 1974.

37. **Mise au point**
Paris: Editions Forces Vives, 1966.

38. **Les Maternelles vous parlent.**
Paris: Gonthier-Denoël, 1968.
Translated into German under the title "Kinder der Strahlenden Stadt," Stuttgart: Verlag Gerd Hatje, and Teufen: Arthur Niggli, 1968.
Translated into English under the title "The Nursery Schools" by Eleanor Levieux, New York: The Orion Press, 1968.

Index

PHOTO CREDITS